Copyright © 2022 Jade Jia Ying Wu

Written by	Jade Jia Ying Wu
Edited by	Edmond Xu, Carmen Yeung
Copy-edited by	Kimberly Newell
Illustration by	Tina Gee
Design by	June Pham
Voice Recording by	Jade Jia Ying Wu, Edmond Xu
Cover Design by	Tina Gee, June Pham

All rights reserved. This book was self-published by the author Jade Jia Ying Wu under Inspirlang Press.

Portions of this book first appeared on the author's website, Inspirlang (www.Inspirlang.com).

Without limiting the rights under the copyright reserved above, no part of this publication may be reproduced, distributed, stored in, or introduced into a retrieval system, or transmitted in any form, or by any means (electronic, mechanical, photocopying, recording, or otherwise), without the written permission of the copyright owner, except in the case of brief quotations embodied in critical reviews and certain other noncommercial uses permitted by the copyright law. For permission requests, contact the author Jade Jia Ying Wu with "Attention: Permissions Coordinator" in the email heading, at the address below.

Jade.Wu@Inspirlang.com

Printed in the United States of America
First Printing, 2022
ISBN-13: 978-0-9996946-6-4

To my grandma Ngin-Ngin, who showed me that
love surpasses languages.
Don't worry if you can't remember anymore.
I will teach you the way you taught me.

Table of Contents

Message from the Author — 6

Features of This Book — 8

Introduction to Taishanese — 10

Crash Course 101 on Taishanese Romanization — 11

Avatars — 16

Chapter 1: *I am ...* — 18
    Chapter 1 Exercises — 26
    Answer Key — 116

Chapter 2: *I want to ...* — 27
    Chapter 2 Exercises — 34
    Answer Key — 116

Chapter 3: *I like to watch ...* — 35
    Chapter 3 Exercises — 44
    Answer Key — 116

Part I Review — 45
    Answer Key — 116

Chapter 4: *Today is ...* — 47
    Chapter 4 Exercises — 55
    Answer Key — 117

Chapter 5: *My Chinese Zodiac Sign is ...* — 56
    Chapter 5 Exercises — 65
    Answer Key — 117

Chapter 6: *I don't feel well*   66
    Chapter 6 Exercises   73
    Answer Key   117-118

Part II Review   75
    Answer Key   118

Chapter 7: *Taking … medicine*   77
    Chapter 7 Exercises   85
    Answer Key   118

Chapter 8: *I am in …*   87
    Chapter 8 Exercises   94
    Answer Key   118

Chapter 9: *How much is …?*   95
    Chapter 9 Exercises   103
    Answer Key   119

Part III Review   105
    Answer Key   119

Chapter 10: *Journaling: past, present, and future*   107
    Chapter 10 Exercises   114
    Answer Key   119

List of Interrogative Pronouns   115

References   120

Acknowledgements   121

About the Author   123

Message from the Author

Six years ago, a friend from a business class mentioned that he was interested in learning Chinese. Since I know Chinese, I told him that I could teach him. That same day, I went home and created a website called Inspirlang, and began creating podcasts, videos, and other digital content to teach Cantonese and Mandarin to non-native speakers. A year later, I wanted to make the same material in Taishanese, so that my cousin—who was struggling to communicate with our family members—could learn from those contents. Little did I know that this small seed would one day turn into the book that you are reading now.

Growing up, I never would have imagined that I'd be advocating for language preservation. As a matter of fact, I only started teaching Taishanese because I saw a need to do so—my cousin and many of my friends were never able to fully understand their parents' and grandparents' words, even at a very basic level. It was shocking and painful for me to see. And I knew the reason why as a language Taishanese struggled more than any other mainstream dialects—many people think it is useless to learn Taishanese, because most Chinese speakers know either Cantonese or Mandarin.

This is not true.

Even with the Chinese government's effort to promote Mandarin, Taishanese is still widely spoken in overseas Chinese communities and within Taishan. Inside a Taishanese family, members still speak exclusively in Taishanese. The reason is very simple. One, Chinese is very different from English and it is more natural for Taishanese elders to speak in their mother tongue. And, two, why not? Speaking your native tongue at home and using a second language outside do not conflict with one another. Rather, it preserves the cultural value of diverse dialects and allows children to acquire a second language more easily. For this reason, Taishanese deserves its full recognition among Taishanese families even amid a time when Mandarin is prevalent. The popularity of Mandarin has certainly added great convenience among Chinese speakers from different regions, and we should acknowledge that. However, we don't have to depreciate one language to lift up another, and instead we can celebrate the diversity of dialects we are able to inherit.

This has inspired me to teach Taishanese through the voice of this book's main character, Amy. Amy's maternal grandmother, Popo, has been suffering from Alzheimer's disease and thus experienced considerable memory loss. As a result, she can no longer speak the other languages she once knew and can only remember her native tongue, Taishanese. The story takes place in San Francisco in the U.S., and most of the scenes described in this book come from spending time with a friend's mother who suffered from Alzheimer's, as well as my own grandmother's experience with dementia. As this book creates a unique bond between me and my grandmother, I hope that it will also bring you closer to your Taishanese friends and family members when you read it.

You will be learning one of the world's most difficult languages, but the most meaningful things in the world are rarely easy. When you give a simple greeting to your friends or family in Taishanese, or place your first order in Taishanese at a restaurant in Chinatown, you can celebrate just how much closer you have gotten to someone's heart.

[hog3 mu4 ji2 gen2]
學無止境
Learning is an endless process.

As this ancient Chinese proverb points out, there is no limit to what you can learn, and it is never too late to start learning a new language. So be patient with your language learning and don't give up. Good luck and enjoy your journey of learning Taishanese!

Jade Jia Ying Wu
May 2021

Features of this Book

Before you jump ahead and start reading this book, here are a few important features that you should know about:

Study Goal

The main goal of this book is to help you to converse in day-to-day Taishanese. However, there is a significant difference between spoken Taishanese and written Chinese. After learning everything in the book, you should be able to form sentences that are useful in everyday conversation and write some of the most commonly used characters.

Audio Track

You can download audio tracks that are supplementary to the book at no additional cost at *www.inspirlang.com/resource*. Audio tracks are provided for Vocabulary, Sample Sentences, and Sample Conversation of each chapter. They are all labeled with a 🔊 sign and organized for your convenience.

Online Flashcards

You can review and study all of the new vocabulary covered in the book by visiting *www.inspirlang.com/resource.*

Vocabulary

In each chapter, there are 3 sections of Vocabulary (A, B and C), all of which are related to the main topic. Audio tracks are available online.

Sample Sentences

Similar to Vocabulary, there are 3 sections of Sample Sentences in each chapter, all of which are constructed using the vocabulary in that chapter. Audio tracks are also available.

Recognizing and Writing Chinese Characters

In each chapter, there is a Recognizing Chinese Characters section with 3-5 characters that the reader should learn to recognize because they are related to the chapter topic and are commonly used in Chinese.

Sample Conversations

Sample conversations in each chapter are designed to help the reader learn how to talk to a Taishanese native speaker spontaneously by using the vocabulary and sentence structures learned in the given chapter. This is the last part of the audio track in each chapter.

Cultural Insights

At the end of each chapter, you will learn about some common Taishanese cultural practices, such as sun-drying clothes or making salted fish. That is how you can learn not just about the language, but also about the culture and its people.

Chapter Exercises

After the section on Cultural Insights, you will have a chance to practice what you have learned in a given chapter with a series of chapter exercises. The questions range from grammatical usage to directly translating the sentences. This is the last section of each chapter.

Introduction to Taishanese

Taishanese (台山話), or sometimes romanized as Toisan, Toisanese or Hoisanva, is a dialect that originated from Taishan (台山)—the place that many Chinese immigrants in the U.S. trace their roots to.

Situated along the coast in the south of Guangdong province, Taishan's geography made it very easy for its people to travel to the U.S. by sea. The first wave of Chinese immigrants from Taishan started in 1848, with the pursuit of the California Gold Rush and later the construction of the First Transcontinental Railroad. Until the 1960s, Taishanese was the main dialect spoken across America's Chinatowns. Today, Taishanese can still be heard in every Chinatown. In addition to that, Taishanese is also known as the representative dialect of the Sze Yap region in China, which includes itself and its neighboring counties— Xinhui, Kaiping (Hoiping), and Enping.

How similar is Taishanese to Cantonese?

Both Taishanese and Cantonese belong to the Yue Language Family of Chinese. Even though Mandarin is becoming more and more popular, Cantonese has served as the common dialect among people that speak different dialects of Yue. Stretching only 90 miles from Guangzhou (two hours by bus) and Hong Kong (2.5 hours by bus excluding customs clearance), Taishan has many traditional practices that are similar to that of Guangzhou and Hong Kong, such as the 飲茶 yum cha (dim sum) tradition. Therefore, because Cantonese has served as the common dialect for most regions of Guangdong, many Taishanese speakers can understand Cantonese, but Cantonese speakers do not always understand Taishanese.

Taishanese and Cantonese exhibit very similar sentence structures and vocabulary usage, but they are still two different dialects, and therefore they are not often mutually intelligible. In fact, Taishanese has its own tonal system and unique consonants and vowels that Cantonese doesn't have. However, due to the influence of Cantonese pop culture, the younger generation from Taishan can often speak Cantonese. This might not be the case for the elderly, who lived in an era when the influence of digital media was minimal and traveling between borders wasn't as convenient.

Crash Course 101 on Taishanese Romanization

In Chinese, people usually speak in word pairs instead of individual characters. The combination of word pairs with tones usually tells the audience what the content is about. Chinese is a tonal language, while English is not. A tonal language means that each character has a fixed pitch pattern.

What is the easiest way to understand tones?

Because many characters can be romanized in the same letters, Chinese speakers differentiate the characters by using different pitches. It is the combination of the spelling with the pitch that makes a character complete. For example, the word "present" in English can be pronounced differently to mean "a gift" or "to formally introduce." Although this might be rare in English, it is very common in Chinese, where speakers understand words based on the tones of the word and the context.

Because Chinese has many homophones, with many words that sound alike but have very different meanings, people make jokes and puns around them. Here are two examples of how Chinese sounds can lead to puns:

4 is considered an unlucky number in Chinese.

But why? That is because "four 四 (lhei1)" is nearly homophonous to the word "death 死 (lhei2)." You see that both "four" and "death" have the same spelling of "lhei," and the numbers "1" and "2" coming after "lhei" indicate the tone of the character. From this example, you can see that two characters with the same spelling but different tones can indicate very different meanings. See the audio section of Taishanese Tones on the following pages to read the phonetics and hear the difference between each tone.

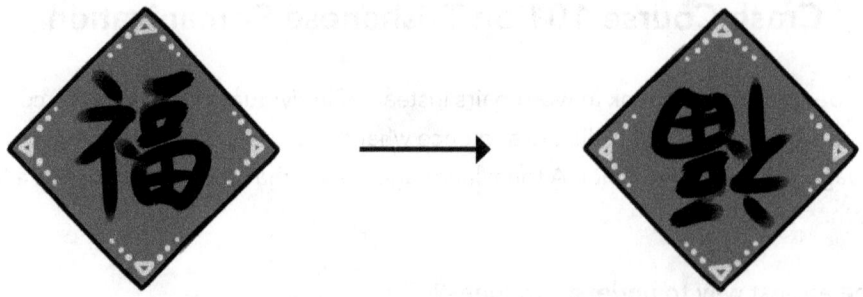

Good fortune "福 (fug2)" character hung upside down

This is a common practice of Chinese New Year. But why? It's because "arrival of good fortune 福到 (fug2 ao1)" sounds exactly the same as "upside down good fortune 福倒 (fug2 ao1)." From this example, you can see that words can have the same pronunciation, yet have different meanings because they are different characters.

How can a non-native speaker tell the difference?

Although Taishanese learning resources are very limited, dedicated researchers have developed different romanization systems to teach Taishanese. In this book, we will use Wu's Phonetic System, a romanization system I developed to help foreign language speakers to enunciate every Chinese character in Taishanese.

What are tones?

Chinese is a tonal language, which means that each character has a fixed pitch pattern. There are 5 tones in Wu's Phonetic System. The digits of 1-5 that appear after the romanized pronunciation indicate the fixed tone of that character. Occasionally you will see two numbers after the English letters, like in the word "sieu1-mai32" for "shiu-mai," a steamed pork dumpling popular at dim sum. This is called a tone change, and it often occurs at the end of a noun phrase and a few other scenarios. Don't worry about that for now, just know that you will see this notation sometimes, but we will dive into this phenomenon later in the second book of this series.

The following sentence includes all five tones in Taishanese:

[ngoi1 ngim2 hang3-ngin4 nai5]
我飲杏仁奶。
I drink almond milk.

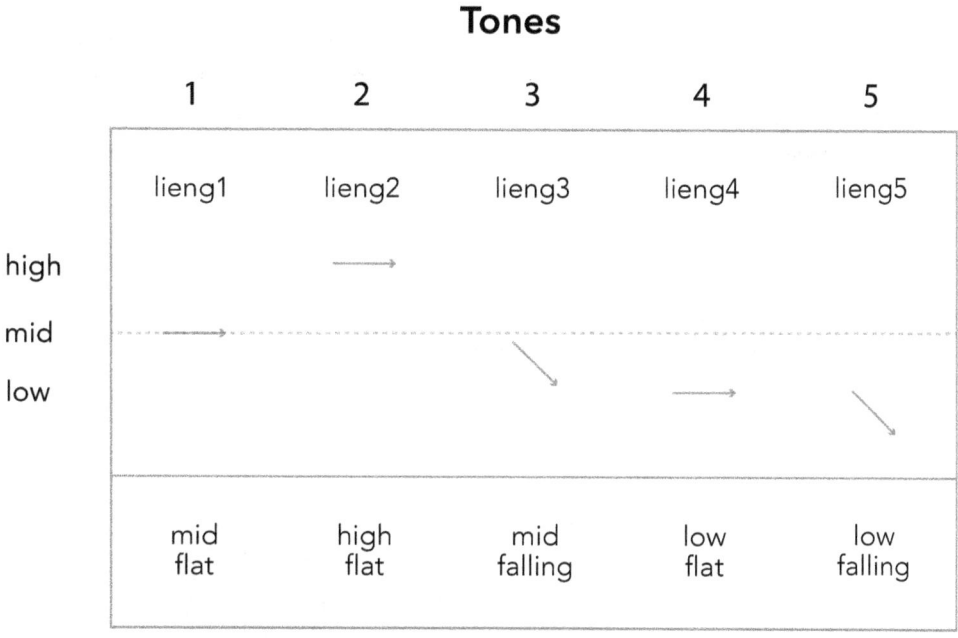

Can't tell the difference from the audio? That is totally fine. This is just for you to know that:
- The numbers above represent different tones
- Different tones indicate different characters
- Different characters can share the same pronunciation and the same tone *(Remember the "good fortune" pun we talked about earlier?)*

This can be tricky because different characters can have the same pronunciation and tone. How can you know when it means one thing and not the other? Usually you can tell from the context and the combination of characters. For example, the sound "ga1" can represent many different characters (including that of my name); however, when it's combined with "fie2," it becomes "ga1-fie2." Then people can tell that it means "coffee."

To make it easier, in this book, multisyllabic words are connected by a dash (-). For example, in "I want to drink coffee (ngoi1 lhieng2 ngim2 ga1-fie2)," ga1-fie2 is connected by a dash because it is considered one word: coffee.

What if I use the wrong tones?

In most cases, people will still be able to understand you even if you can't say the different tones of each character correctly. However, there are times when combinations of the wrong tones can make up different words. Just remember, the more you listen, the easier it will be to tell the difference between tones. The more you speak, the closer you are to saying it correctly. So don't be afraid to try even if you are not sure that you are using the correct tone.

Due to the regional difference among different towns and villages of Taishan, a number of Taishanese accents also developed over time. This book is written based on the accent of Taicheng subdistrict, which is considered the capital level of Taishan.

> If the Taishanese you speak sounds a little different from this book, you might just be speaking a different accent, or topolect of Taishanese and they are both valid!

Wu's Phonetic System Initials

(in comparison to English pronunciation)

b **b**oy	p **p**ie	m **m**ike	f **f**ive	d **d**og	t **t**om	n **n**ice	l **l**ight	g **g**o	k **k**ind
h **h**ot	ng ha**ng**	j **j**oy	c **c**ants	s **s**ing	lh *	v **v**iolin	y **y**es		

	-	b	d	g	i	m	n	ng	o	u
a	a 啊 [a3] ouch	ab 鴨 [ab12] duck	ad 押 [ad1] detain	ag 賊 [tag3] thief	ai 矮 [ai2] short	am 啱 [ngam2] correct	an 晏 [an1] late	ang 等 [ang2] wait	ao 奧 [ao1] mysterious	
e	e 誒 [e1] ...ed	eb 磕 [keb1] kowtow	ed 跌 [ed1] to fall		ei 偉 [vei2] great	em 鵪 [em1] quail	en 清 [ten1] light			eu 歐 [eu1] Europe
i	i 依 [yi1] rely	ib 入 [yib3] enter	id 七 [tid2] seven			im 音 [yim1] music	in 印 [yin1] print			iu 休 [hiu1] rest
ie	ie 嘢 [yie1] thing	ieb 碟 [ieb3] plate		ieg 踢 [pieg1] to kick				ieng 唱 [cieng1] sing		ieu 椒 [dieu1] pepper
o	o 哦 [o3] oh		od 乜 [mod2] what	og 惡 [og2] evil	oi 愛 [oi1] love		on 安 [on1] peace	ong 當 [ong1] pretend		
u	u 布 [bu1] fabric		ud 突 [ud3] protrude	ug 屋 [ug2] house	ui 對 [ui1] to		un 溫 [vun1] warm	ung 凍 [ung1] cold	uo 多 [uo1] many	
						m 唔 [m4] not		ng 五 [ng2] five		

*Similar to th- but instead of the tongue on the teeth, it's closer to the roof of the mouth. Use a little more air than usual, almost like you are blowing out a candle without pursing your lips

Avatars

My name is Amy, and I aspire to become a children's book writer. Some of my earliest memories are of my grandmother, Popo, trying to teach me Taishanese. Growing up in San Francisco, Popo always spoke Taishanese to me, though I wasn't always ready to reply in the same language, except for some food names.

In my second year of college, Popo's Alzheimer's disease had progressed to the point where she forgot the people she used to love. Devastated by the fact that I might never be able to connect with Popo the way I used to do, I decided to take Taishanese classes at Inspirlang and move into Popo's Chinatown apartment that summer to spend more time with her. It was truly the best decision I made in my life.

To my right is my grandmother, Popo. She is 81 years old and loves dancing. She arrived in San Francisco's Chinatown as a refugee from Vietnam and has lived there ever since. When I was young, I always went to her apartment after school, where she cooked me the most delicious food that I couldn't find anywhere else. I later discovered that those were all Taishanese delicacies. Before the passing of my grandpa and her Alzheimer's disease diagnosis, she was the most joyous and playful woman I ever knew. Even as her Alzheimer's severely progressed and she forgot most of her family, she knew that I was a safe harbor for her.

The last and only thing I could do for her was to learn Taishanese so that I could understand the only words she had left and pass down her legacy.

Chapter 1

I am ...
我係...
(ngoi1 hai3 ...)

In this chapter, I am revisiting the family photo album with Grandma to remind her of the family members that she once loved dearly. Although Alzheimer's might cause Grandma to forget our names within minutes, I still want to treasure each minute I spend with her to let her know how deeply she is loved in the present moment.

我 [ngoi1] = I; me
係 [hai3] = am, are, is; yes
我 [ngoi1] + 係 [hai3] + name = I am ...
你 [nei1] = you

好 [hao2] = good; well; very
你 [nei1] + 好 [hao2] = hello

As you can see, the way people greet each other in Chinese is similar to saying, "You are well," in English. Although 你好 (nei1-hao2) is the official way to greet someone, the Chinese diaspora usually greets one another using the less formal "hello" in English.

Vocabulary A 🔊

屋企人 [ug2-kei2 ngin4] = Family Members			
	Singular	Possessive	Plural Pronouns & Possessive Pronouns
Singular	我 [ngoi1] I	我嘅 [ngoi1 ge1] my	偃 [ngoi5] we; our
Second Person	你 [nei1] you	你嘅 [nei1 ge1] your	偌 [nieg5] you; your
Third Person	佢 [kui1] he; she; it	佢嘅 [kui1 ge1] his; her; its	御 [kieg5] they; their

Sample Sentences A 🔊

我係 Janice。 [ngoi1 hai3 Janice]
I am Janice.

你好，我係 David。 [nei1-hao2, ngoi1 hai3 David]
Hello, I am David.

佢係 Kevin。 [kui1 hai3 Kevin]
He is Kevin.

佢係 Jason。[kui1 hai3 Jason]
He is Jason.

佢係婷婷。[kui1 hai3 hen4-hen42]
She is Ting-Ting. *(named romanized in Mandarin)*

我唔係婷婷。[ngoi1 m4 hai3 hen4-hen42]
I am not Ting-Ting.

Tips: As you can see, 唔 (m4) is used as "not" to negate a sentence.

你唔係我。[nei1 m4 hai3 ngoi1]
You are not me.

佢唔係偉明。[kui1 m4 hai3 vei2-men4]
He is not Wei-Ming.

Vocabulary B 🔊

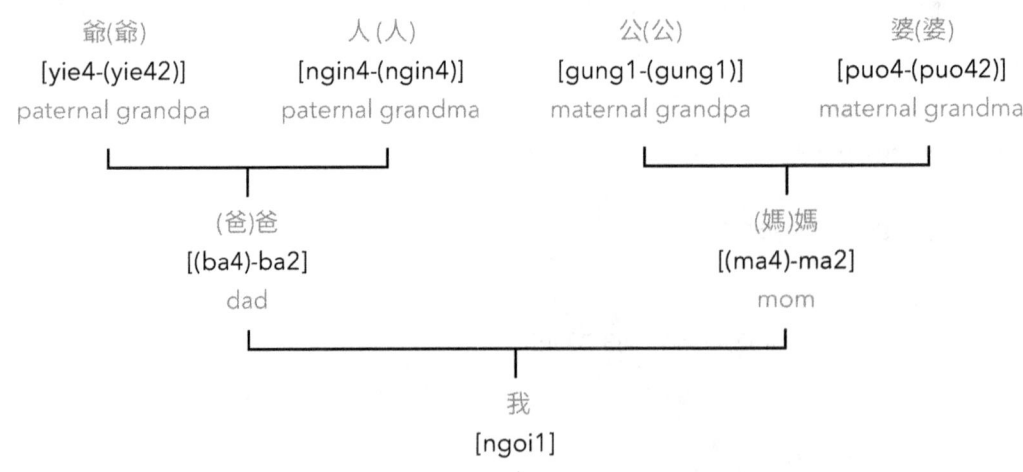

爺(爺)
[yie4-(yie42)]
paternal grandpa

人(人)
[ngin4-(ngin4)]
paternal grandma

公(公)
[gung1-(gung1)]
maternal grandpa

婆(婆)
[puo4-(puo42)]
maternal grandma

(爸)爸
[(ba4)-ba2]
dad

(媽)媽
[(ma4)-ma2]
mom

我
[ngoi1]

While you can also address your family without the second character in the parenthesis, such as 阿爺 (a1 yie4), 阿婆 (a1 puo4), and 阿媽 (a1 ma2), repeating the second character is a more intimate way to address the person.

Sample Sentences B 🔊

婆婆,你好。[puo4-puo42, nei1-hao2]
Hi, Grandma.

佢係我嘅媽媽。[kui1 hai3 ngoi1 ge1 ma4-ma2]
She is my mom.

佢係偓媽。[kui1 hai3 ngoi5 ma2]
She is my/our mom.

你係偓人。[nei1 hai3 ngoi5 ngin4]
You are my/our (paternal) grandma.

佢係偌公。[kui1 hai3 nieg5 gung1]
He is your (maternal) grandpa.

我係御爸。[ngoi1 hai3 kieg5 ba2]
I am their dad.

佢唔係御爺爺。[kui1 m4 hai3 kieg5 yie4-yie42]
He is not their (paternal) grandpa.

As you can see, when you use a possessive pronoun (i.e. ngoi5), you can use the simplified version of 媽媽 (ma4-ma2) by just using 媽 (ma2).

Vocabulary C 🔊

兄弟姐妹 [hen1-ai3 dei2-moi5] = siblings*

*Literal meaning: older brother - younger brother - older sister - younger sister

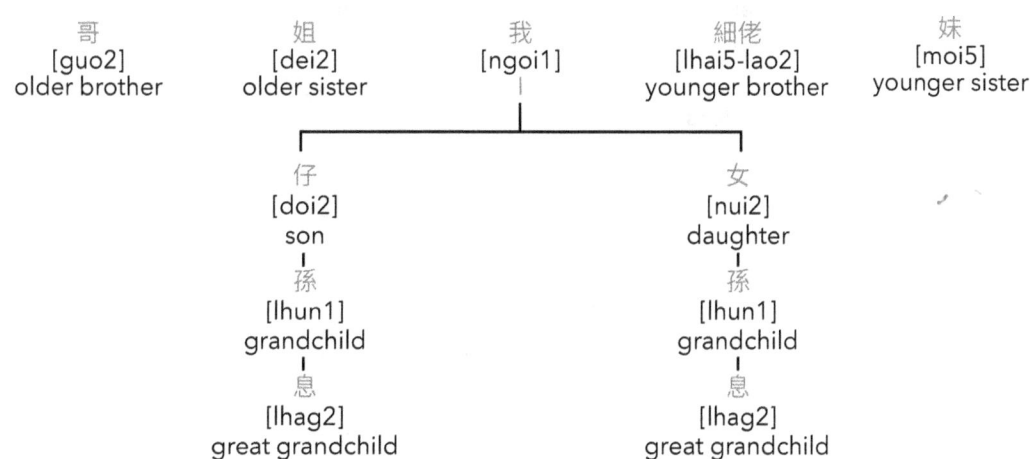

Sample Sentences C

我係你嘅孫。[ngoi1 hai3 nei1 ge1 lhun1]
I am your grandchild.

> 我嘅 [ngoi1 ge1] = my
> 你嘅 [nei1 ge1] = your
> 佢嘅 [kui1 ge1] = his/hers/its

你係我嘅妹。[nei1 hai3 ngoi1 ge1 moi5]
You are my younger sister.

我係你嘅仔。[ngoi1 hai3 nei1 ge1 doi2]
I am your son.

佢係你嘅息。[kui1 hai3 nei1 ge1 lhag32]
He/she is your great grandchild.

你係唔係佢嘅女? [nei1 hai3 m4 hai3 kui1 ge1 nui2?]
Are you his/her daughter?

佢唔係俉細佬，我冇細佬。[kui1 m4 hai3 ngoi5 lhai5-lao2, ngoi1 mao1 lhai5-lao2]
He is not my younger brother; I don't have any younger brothers.
冇 (mao1) = to not have

As you see, the 冇 (mao1) character, which means that one "doesn't have", doesn't include the lines inside the 有 (yiu1) character.

Recognizing Chinese Characters

你 [nei1] = you
我 [ngoi1] = I
公 [gung1] = maternal grandpa

Sample Conversation 🔊

Amy

婆婆，俺睇相呀。
[puo4-puo42, ngoi5 hai2 lhieng12 ya4]
Grandma, let's take a look at the photos.

Grandma

哦。[o5]
Okay.

Amy

佢係你嘅仔，佢係你嘅女。
[kui1 hai3 nei1 ge1 doi2, kui1 hai3 nei1 ge1 nui2]
He is your son, (and) she is your daughter.

A beginner's guide to mastering conversational Taishanese

你係我嘅女？[nei1 hai3 ngoi1 ge1 nui2?]
You are my daughter?

Grandma

Amy

我係你嘅孫。
[ngoi1 hai3 nei1 ge1 lhun1]
I am your grandchild.

你係誰啊？[nei1 hai3 sui52 a1?]
Who are you (again)?

Grandma

Amy

我係Amy。
[ngoi1 hai3 Amy]
I am Amy.

Remember, the best way to share love with a family member who has dementia is by showing patience and compassion. There are many cases in which dementia patients live in their past memories and revert to their first languages.

Cultural Insights | Multiple Generations Living in the Same Household

In traditional settings, it is very common for three generations of family members to live together, both for cultural and financial reasons. To a traditional Chinese family, being able to take care of the elderly is a blessing, which has made nursing homes and home aides unpopular in China. In Chinese, there is also a phrase 養兒防老 (yieng1 ngei4 fong4 lao2), which means, "Rearing children prevents one from aging."

In major cities like Beijing, each square meter starts from 50,000 yuan, or about $7,700USD. According to *The Wall Street Journal*, as of June 2021, a modest apartment in Shenzhen (130 miles from Taishan) costs more than $1 million. Therefore, it is very conventional for newlyweds to live with their in-laws. Furthermore, most of today's young adults grew up with the one-child policy and have no siblings to share their parents' house with.

Not every Chinese couple is as traditional nowadays. With the strong influence of Western values, the younger Chinese generation also yearns for more privacy. Therefore, most couples would rather find a space of their own, unless they are financially restrained.

Chapter 1 Exercises

1. What is the literal meaning of "你好 (nei1-hao2)" in Chinese?

   _____

2. Translate or transliterate the following sentences:

   佢係俉媽。[kui1 hai3 ngoi5 ma2]

   _____

   我係你嘅女。[____ ____ ____ ____ ____]
   I am your daughter.

   你唔係俉爸。[nei1 m4 hai3 kieg5 ba2]

   _____

   佢係倨細佬。[kui1 hai3 nieg5 lhai5-lao2]

   _____

Chapter 2

I want to …
我想...
(ngoi1 lhieng2 …)

It is such a lovely day outside today, so I decided to bring Popo to her favorite dim sum restaurant in San Francisco's Chinatown – Lai Hong Lounge. In this chapter, I am ordering different types of food from the dim sum cart that Popo used to like. After reading this chapter, you will be able to order food at a Chinese restaurant and become familiar with some Chinese dining etiquette.

想 [lhieng2] = to want to ...

攞 [huo2] = to get ...

想攞 [lhieng2 huo2] = to want to get ...; would like ...

我 [ngoi1] + 想攞 [lhieng2 huo2] + noun = I would like + noun

Vocabulary A 🔊

蝦餃 [ha5-gao2] = shrimp dumpling

燒賣 [sieu1-mai32] = shiu-mai; steamed dumpling

蝦腸 [ha5-cieng42] = shrimp rice noodle roll

粥 [jug2] = congee

 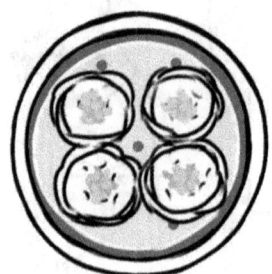 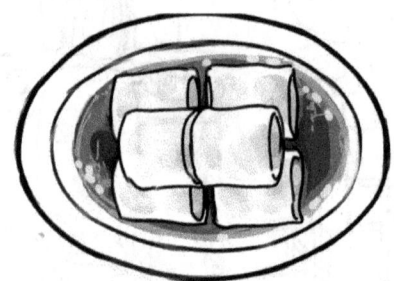

Sample Sentences A 🔊

我想攞蝦餃。[ngoi1 lhieng2 huo2 ha5-gao2]
I would like (a serving of) shrimp dumplings.

我想攞燒賣。[ngoi1 lhieng2 huo2 sieu1-mai32]
I would like (a serving of) shiu-mai.

我想攞粥。[ngoi1 lhieng2 huo2 jug2]
I would like (a serving of) congee.

我想攞蝦腸。[ngoi1 lhieng2 huo2 ha5-cieng42]
I would like (a serving of) shrimp rice noodle rolls.

Tip: "我想攞... (ngoi1 lhieng2 huo2)" is simply a general way of telling the waiter what you would like to order; however, at most dim sum restaurants, you will have to walk up to the dim sum cart to place your order.

唔該 [m4-goi1] = excuse me (for attention); thank you (for service)

唔該，我想攞… [m4-goi1, ngoi1 lhieng2 huo2 …] = Excuse me, I would like …

> **Tip:** Remember, you can always use 唔該 (m4-goi1) when you want to say "excuse me" to get someone's attention or to thank the other person for any service that he/she has done for you. However, 唔該 (m4-goi1) cannot be used when someone gives you a compliment or a gift. You will learn more about other ways of saying "thank you" in Chapter 9 later.

Vocabulary B 🔊

飲 [ngim2] = to drink

茶 [ca4] = tea

水 [sui2] = water

咖啡 [ga1-fie2] = coffee

奶茶 [nai5-ca4] = milk tea

涼茶 [lieng4-ca4] = herbal tea

普洱 [pu2-nei32] = Pu'er tea

菊普 [gug2-pu2] = Pu'er with chrysanthemum

Sample Sentences B 🔊

唔該，我想攞茶。[m4-goi1, ngoi1 lhieng2 huo2 ca4]
Excuse me, I would like some tea.

唔該，我想攞水。[m4-goi1, ngoi1 lhieng2 huo2 sui2]
Excuse me, I would like some water.

佢想飲水。[kui1 lhieng2 ngim2 sui2]
He/she wants to drink water.

你要飲涼茶。[nei1 yieu1 ngim2 lieng4-ca4]
You have to drink herbal tea.

我想飲茶。[ngoi1 lhieng2 ngim2 ca4]
I want to drink tea. OR I want to have dim sum.

In Taishanese and Cantonese, "飲茶 [ngim2-ca4] drinking tea" usually has the implication of "to have dim sum." To differentiate whether it means literally "to drink tea" or its implied meaning of "to have dim sum," pay attention to the context.

Vocabulary C 🔊

乜 [mod2] = what
糍 [tei4] = traditional Chinese cake
糍仔 [tei4-doi2] = Taishanese-style munchkin
鹹糍 [ham4-tei42] = taro cake (similar to Cantonese 芋頭糕 [wu5-tau2 gou1])
發粿 [fad1-gao52] = Taishanese cupcake
雞籠 [gai1-lung52] = deep fried crispy pork dumpling (Cantonese 咸水角 [haam4-seoi2-gok3])
鹹魚 [ham4-ngui5] = salted fish
臘腸 [lab3-cieng42] = Chinese preserved sausage
黃鱔飯 [vong4-sen5 fan3] = yellow eel (clay pot) rice

Table Fact 1: Subject-Verb-Object (S.V.O.) is the most basic sentence structure in Chinese. As you may have noticed, all of the examples that we have encountered so far are simple statements that fall into the subject-verb-object pattern, and they are very similar to English. However, in sentences with interrogative words (who, what, when, where, why, which, how), the most basic pattern becomes subject-verb-*question-word*. You can take a look at the example below.

Sample Sentences C 🔊

你 [nei1] + 想 [lhieng2] + 攞 [huo2] + 乜 [mod2] ? = What would you like?
(word-for-word translation: You want to get what?)

Now, let's explore some traditional Taishanese delicacies that Popo used to enjoy.

Recognizing Chinese Characters

水 [sui2] = water
茶 [ca4] = tea
奶 [nai5] = milk

Sample Conversation

Amy

婆婆，你想吃乜啊？
[puo4-puo42, nei1 lhieng2 hieg1 mod2 a1?]
Popo, what do you want to eat?

我乜都吃。[ngoi1 mod2 du2 hieg1]
I can eat anything.

Grandma

Auntie

婆婆鍾意吃燒賣。
[puo4-puo42 jung1-yi1 hieg1 sieu1-mai32]
Popo likes to eat shiu-mai.

唔該，我想攞燒賣。
[m4-goi1, ngoi1 lhieng2 huo2 sieu1-mai32]
Excuse me, I would like shiu-mai.

Amy

A beginner's guide to mastering conversational Taishanese

哦。[o5]
Okay.

Server

唔該。好吃嗎，婆婆？
[m4-goi1. hao2-hieg1 ma1, puo4-puo42?]
Thank you. Is it delicious, Popo?

Amy

好好吃。[hao2 hao2-hieg1]
(It's) very delicious.

Grandma

Cultural Insights | Taishanese Specialty Food

Located along the coast in the south of Guangdong province, Taishan has the advantage of access to a wide range of seafood. Along with 鹹魚 (ham4-ngui5) salted fish, sun-dried foods became very common in the Taishanese community as a way to preserve seafood prior to modern refrigeration. Another Taishanese specialty food is salted shrimp paste, 鹹蝦醬 (ham4 ha5 dieng1), which is typically shortened to ham4-ma5 when the final "m" in "ham4" is carried over to the next character.

Why do people eat salted fish?
Salted fish is generally consumed in small portions and is a common food at Cantonese dinner tables. In particular, Taishanese elders love salted fish because it was once considered an indulgence during times when food was scarce and every family had a strict ration of meat consumption. The pros and cons of eating salted fish is still controversial.

Chapter 2 Exercises

1. What can you say as "thank you" when someone does something for you?

   _____

2. What can you say as "excuse me" to get someone's attention?

   _____

3. What is missing from this sentence?

   [nei1_____ _____ mod2?] = What would you like?

4. Translate or transliterate the following sentences:

   [ngoi1 lhieng2 huo2 ha5-gao2]
   我想攞蝦餃。

   _____

   [nei1 lhieng2 huo2 sieu1-mai32?]
   你想攞燒賣?

   _____

5. Fill in the blanks.

   A: 你想攞乜? [nei1 lhieng2 huo2 _____?]

   B: 我想攞茶。[_____ _____ _____ ca4]
      I would like (some) tea.

Chapter 3

I like to watch …
我鍾意睇…
(ngoi1 jung1-yi1 hai2 …)

As Grandma's Alzheimer's disease has progressed, she has started to have trouble expressing what she loves to do. The best way to find out is by spending time with her!

In this chapter, we bond incredibly well while watching recorded performances from Grandma's favorite singer: Teresa Teng. I am very thrilled to see how passionate and romantic Grandma is even in the midst of her Alzheimer's. We dance, clap our hands, and communicate in ways that we never have in the past.

After reading this chapter, you will be able to tell others what you like to do as a hobby and ask others what their favorite pastimes are.

Vocabulary A 🔊

鍾意 [jung1-yi1] = to like

該個 [koi5-goi1] = this (one)

嗶個 [nen5-goi1] = that (one)

In Chinese, a classifier, or measure word, is needed to quantify or specify amounts. This is analogous to the "bottle" in the phrase "a bottle of water," the "piece" in "two pieces of paper," and "pound" in "three pounds of beef." There are many classifiers in Chinese, and they are usually classified by a specific category such as shape and functionality. However, the generic classifier that we have been using so far is 個 (goi1), which can be used for people and abstract things. Right now, let us first get used to the generic classifier 個 (goi1).

Sample Sentences A 🔊

我鍾意該個。[ngoi1 jung1-yi1 koi5-goi1]
I like this one.

我鍾意嗶個。[ngoi1 jung1-yi1 nen5-goi1]
I like that one.

我好鍾意嗶個。[ngoi1 hao2 jung1-yi1 nen5-goi1]
I really like that one.

你鍾意佢。[nei1 jung1-yi1 kui1]
You like him/her/it.

你鍾意佢嗎? [nei1 jung1-yi1 kui1 ma1?]
Do you like him/her/it?

我鍾意你。[ngoi1 jung1-yi1 nei1]
I like you.

我好鍾意你。[ngoi1 hao2 jung1-yi1 nei1]
I really like you. / I love you.

Cultural Insights | How do people express affection in Chinese?

In Chinese, people rarely say, "I love you" to close friends, family members, and even romantic partners. Saying, "Love you" or, "Miss you" to friends can be a little awkward. You will also hear partners say, "I really like you 我好鍾意你 (ngoi1 hao2 jung1-yi1 nei1)," instead of, "I love you 我愛你 (ngoi1 oi1 nei1)."

To express affection to family members, you often hear the word 錫 (sieg1), which means to "spoil." For example, 偓爺爺好錫我 (ngoi5 yie4-yie42 hao2 sieg1 ngoi1), "My paternal grandpa spoils me a lot."

Now let's explore some verbs to find out what Grandma enjoys.

Vocabulary B 🔊

睇 [hai2] = to read; to watch

睇書 [hai2 si1] = to read books

睇電視 [hai2 en3-si3] = to watch TV

聽 [hieng1] = to listen; to hear

聽音樂 [hieng1 yim1-ngog3] = to listen to music

唱歌 [cieng1-guo52] = to sing

跳舞 [hieu1-mu2] = to dance

做 [du1] = to do

Sample Sentences B 🔊

我鍾意睇書。[ngoi1 jung1-yi1 hai2 si1]
I like to read.

佢鍾意唱歌。[kui1 jung1-yi1 cieng1-guo52]
He/she likes to sing.

你鍾意做乜？[nei1 jung1-yi1 du1 mod2?]
What do you like to do?

我睇佢唱歌。[ngoi1 hai2 kui1 cieng1-guo52]
I watch him/her sing.

我鍾意睇你跳舞。[ngoi1 jung1-yi1 hai2 nei1 hieu1-mu2]
I like to watch you dance.

佢鍾意睇乜書？[kui1 jung1-yi1 hai2 mod2 si1?]
What books does he/she like to read?

你鍾意聽乜音樂？[nei1 jung1-yi1 hieng1 mod2 yim1-ngog3?]
What music do you like to listen to?

你鍾意睇乜電視？ [nei1 jung1-yi1 hai2 mod2 en3-si3?]
What TV (shows) do you like to watch?

As you might realize, even with Alzheimer's, Grandma is eager to express her opinions. Let's dive into her words to learn about her preferences.

Vocabulary C 🔊

靚 [lieng1] = pretty

飽 [bao2] = full

眼瞓 [ngan2-fun1] = sleepy

劼 [gui3] = tired

爽 [song2] = to have a good time

好好 [hao2 hao2] = very good

好聽 [hao2-hieng12] = melodious (Word-for-word translation: pleasant to listen to)

好睇 [hao2-hai2] = fun to read (Word-for-word translation: pleasant to read/watch)

Sample Sentences C 🔊

我好飽。[ngoi1 hao2 bao2]
I am very full.

該個好好。[koi5-goi1 hao2 hao2]
This one is very good.

該個好好睇。[koi5-goi1 hao2 hao2-hai2]
This is fun to watch/read.

該個好睇嗎？[koi5-goi1 hao2-hai2 ma1?]
Is this fun to watch?

佢唱歌好聽嗎？[kui1 cieng1-guo52 hao2-hieng12 ma1?]
Does he/she sing well?

> As you can see, to form a yes/no question, you can add the final particle 嗎 (ma1) at the end of your original statement. For example, if "佢眼瞓 (kui1 ngan2-fun1) he is sleepy" is the original statement, its corresponding yes/no question is "佢眼瞓嗎？(kui1 ngan2-fun1 ma1?) is he sleepy?"

A beginner's guide to mastering conversational Taishanese

你眼瞓嗎? [nei1 ngan2-fun1 ma1?]
Are you sleepy?

我好劼。[ngoi1 hao2 gui3]
I am very tired.

你劼嗎? [nei1 gui3 ma1?]
Are you tired?

Recognizing Chinese Characters

好 [hao2] = very; good
音 [yim1] = sound
個 [goi1] = is a generic classifier for objects and ideas

Sample Conversation 🔊

Amy

婆婆，你想睇乜？
[puo4-puo42, nei1 lhieng2 hai2 mod2?]
Grandma, what do you want to watch?

Grandma: 睇該個。[hai2 koi5-goi1]
(Let's) watch this.

Amy: 你鍾意佢嗎？
[nei1 jung1-yi1 kui1 ma1?]
Do you like her?

Grandma: 佢好靚。[kui1 hao2 lieng1]
She is very pretty.

Amy: 係啊。偓跳舞啦！
[hai3 a1. ngoi5 hieu1-mu2 la2!]
Yes. Let's dance!

Grandma: 哦。[o5]
Okay.

Amy: 你鍾意跳舞嗎？
[nei1 jung1-yi1 hieu1-mu2 ma1?]
Do you like to dance?

Grandma: 鍾意。[jung1-yi1]
Yes. (I like to).

Amy

爽嗎？
[song2 ma1?]
Are you having a good time?

爽。[song2]
Yes. (I'm having a good time).

Grandma

Cultural Insights | Cantonese Operas and Gender Representation

Chinese operas started with emperor Li Longji from the Tang Dynasty (618-907 A.D.). In Chinese opera, cross-gender acting is a very common practice. Gender roles are usually disguised under heavy makeup and costumes.

There are 360 types of Chinese opera, with Peking Opera and Cantonese Opera as two of the most well-known ones. The biggest difference between Peking Opera and Cantonese Opera is the language spoken in each. Mandarin is generally used in a Peking Opera while Cantonese is used in a Cantonese Opera.

Understanding the context of a Chinese opera show usually requires some knowledge of the historical background. It is not nearly as popular as it once was when it was one of the few modes of entertainment before TV, streaming, and movies. In addition, Chinese operas are often labeled as a pastime for "old people." To preserve the invaluable cultural heritage of Chinese opera, such labels should be abandoned.

See answers on page #116

Chapter 3 Exercises

1. How do you express what you like to do?
   _____

2. What do you add at the end of a sentence to change a statement into a yes/no question?
   _____

3. How do you ask someone, "What do you like to do?"
   _____

4. Transliterate or translate the following sentences:

   我好眼瞓。[_____ _____ _____ _____]
   I am very sleepy.

   我鍾意睇書。[ngoi1 jung1-yi1 hai2 si1]

   _____

   你鍾意跳舞嗎? [nei1 jung1-yi1 hieu1-mu2 ma1?]

   _____

   你鍾意聽乜音樂? [_____ _____ _____ _____ _____ _____ _____?]
   What music do you like to listen to?

Part I Review

- To greet another person, you say, "你好 (nei1-hao2) hello."
- To tell someone what your name is, you say, "我係... (ngoi1 hai3 ...) I am ...."
- To negate, you add "唔 (m4) not" before the verb.
- Possessive form is: pronoun + 嘅 (ge1)
- To order at a restaurant or cafe, you can say, "我想攞... (ngoi1 lhieng2 huo2) I would like ...."
- To ask for someone's attention, you say, "唔該 (m4-goi1) excuse me."
- To thank someone for the service they have done for you, you can also say, "唔該 (m4-goi1) thank you."
- To say something "is very ...," you use 好 (hao2).
- To express that the food is very delicious, you can say, "好好吃 (hao2 hao2-hieg1) very delicious."
- To express that you like something, you can say, "我鍾意...(ngoi1 jung1-yi1 ...) I like ...."
- This = 該個 (koi5-goi1)
- That = 嗰個 (nen5-goi1)

Sample Paragraph

你好, 我係陳美。我鍾意聽音樂, 唔鍾意唱歌。我好想吃蝦餃同粥。
[nei1-hao2, ngoi1 hai3 cin4 mei5. ngoi1 jung1-yi1 hieng1 yim1-ngog3, m4 jung1-yi1 cieng1-guo52. ngoi1 hao2 lhieng2 hieg1 ha5-gao2 hung4 jug2]
Hi, my name is May Chin. I like to listen to music (and) don't like to sing. I really want to eat shrimp dumplings and congee.

Sample Exercises

Translate or transliterate the following sentences.

1. [kui1 hai3 ngoi5 ma2]

2. [ngoi1 lhieng2 huo2 ha5-cieng42]

   _____

3. I am very tired.
   [_____ _____ _____]

Chapter 4

Today is ...
今日係...
(gim1-ngid5 hai3 ...)

When your loved one with Alzheimer's gets confused about who you are and has trouble expressing themselves, you wouldn't be surprised if their recognition of numbers becomes minimal, or is completely lost. That is why it is more crucial than ever to have Grandma practice with numbers now before she loses them completely.

In this chapter, Popo and I practice saying phone numbers and days of the week by going through basic numbers. To me, it might be a lot of repetition, but to Grandma, every mention of the numbers refreshes her memory. After reading this chapter, you will be able to freely use numbers from the number 0-10. You will also learn to use time expressions to say the week and day, which are built upon basic cardinal numbers.

Now, let's take a look at the numbers from 0-10.

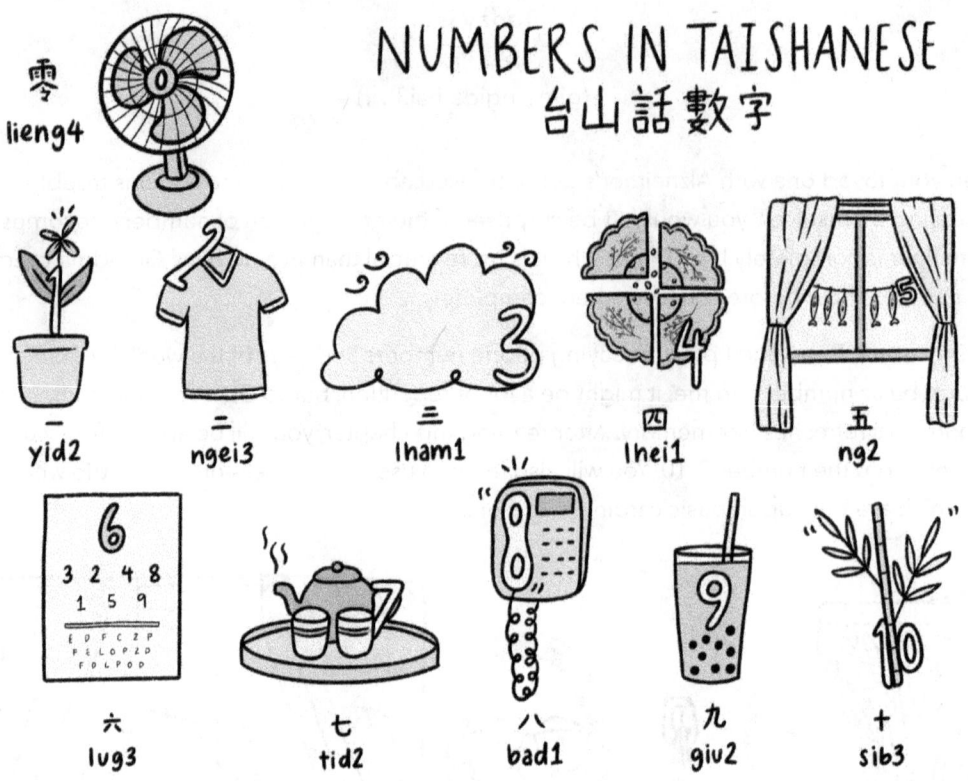

Vocabulary A 🔊

零 [lieng4] = 0
一 [yid2] = 1
二 [ngei3] = 2
三 [lham1] = 3
四 [lhei1] = 4
五 [ng2] = 5
六 [lug3] = 6
七 [tid2] = 7
八 [bad1] = 8
九 [giu2] = 9
十 [sib3] = 10

Sample Sentences A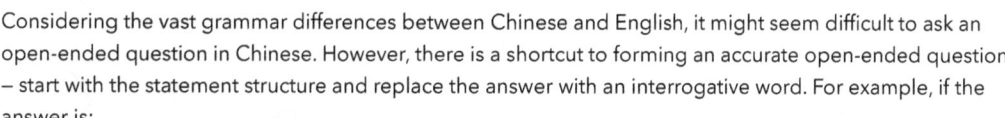

我嘅電話號碼係929-382-4711。
[ngoi1 ge1 en3-va32 hao3-ma52 hai3 giu2-ngei3-giu2, lham1-bad1-ngei3, lhei1-tid2-yid2-yid2]
My phone number is 929-382-4711.

佢嘅電話係746-829-0193。
[kui1 ge1 en3-va32 hai3 tid2-lhei1-lug3, bad1-ngei3-giu2, lieng4-yid2-giu2-lham1]
His/her phone (number) is 746-829-0193.

佢嘅號碼係746-829-0193。
[kui1 ge1 hao3-ma52 hai3 tid2-lhei1-lug3, bad1-ngei3-giu2, lieng4-yid2-giu2-lham1]
His/her (phone) number is 746-829-0193.

我有電話。[ngoi1 yiu1 en3-va32]
I have a phone (number).

我冇電話。[ngoi1 mao1 en3-va32]
I don't have a phone (number).

As you can see, "電話 (en3-va32) phone," "號碼 (hao3-ma52) number," and "電話號碼 (en3-va32 hao3-ma52) phone number" can be used interchangeably to mean "phone number."

你嘅電話號碼係乜?
[nei1 ge1 en3-va32 hao3-ma52 hai3 mod2?]
What is your phone number?*

*Word-for-word translation: Your phone number is what?

> Considering the vast grammar differences between Chinese and English, it might seem difficult to ask an open-ended question in Chinese. However, there is a shortcut to forming an accurate open-ended question — start with the statement structure and replace the answer with an interrogative word. For example, if the answer is:
>
> 我嘅電話號碼係1234567。
> [ngoi1 ge1 en3-va32 hao3-ma52 hai3 yid2 ngei3 lham1 lhei1 ng2 lug3 tid2]
> My phone number is 1234567.
>
> Then your question will be formed as:
> 你嘅電話號碼係乜?
> [nei1 ge1 en3-va32 hao3-ma52 hai3 mod2?]
> Your phone number is what?*

*In English, we would usually say, "What is your phone number?"

A beginner's guide to mastering conversational Taishanese

Now, let's explore the names for the different days of the week.

Vocabulary B 🔊

禮拜 [lai5-bai1] = week

禮拜一 [lai5-bai1-yid2] = Monday (Word-for-word: week, one)

禮拜二 [lai5-bai1-ngei3] = Tuesday (Word-for-word: week, two)

禮拜三 [lai5-bai1-lham1] = Wednesday (Word-for-word: week, three)

禮拜四 [lai5-bai1-lhei1] = Thursday (Word-for-word: week, four)

禮拜五 [lai5-bai1-ng2] = Friday (Word-for-word: week, five)

禮拜六 [lai5-bai1-lug3] = Saturday (Word-for-word: week, six)

禮拜日 [lai5-bai1-ngid52] = Sunday (Word-for-word: week, sun)

禮拜尾 [lai5-bai1-mei2] = weekend (Word-for-word: the tail end of the week)

Sample Sentences B 🔊

我唔鍾意禮拜一。[ngoi1 m4 jung1-yi1 lai5-bai1-yid2]
I don't like Mondays.

係禮拜三。[hai3 lai5-bai1-lham1]
It's Wednesday.

今日係禮拜四。[gim1-ngid5 hai3 lai5-bai1-lhei1]
Today is Thursday.

今日唔係禮拜五。[gim1-ngid5 m4 hai3 lai5-bai1-ng2]
Today is not Friday.

今日係禮拜幾? [gim1-ngid5 hai3 lai5-bai1 gei2?]
What day of the week is today?

禮拜六我飲茶。[lai5-bai1-lug3 ngoi1 ngim2-ca4]
I am having dim sum on Saturday.

> If you are expecting the answer to have a number value, your interrogative word will usually be 幾 (gei2).

禮拜日好嗎？[lai5-bai1-ngid52 hao2 ma1?]
Is Sunday good?

Now that we have learned how to say each day of the week, let's learn how to add more time elements into your sentences to make them more accurate.

Vocabulary C 🔊

昨晚 [dam5-man52] = yesterday
今日 [gim1-ngid5] = today
天早 [hen4-dao2] = tomorrow

早朝 [dao2-jieu5] = morning
晏晝 [an1-jiu5] = afternoon
晚黑 [man5-hag2] = evening

Sample Sentences C 🔊

偓天早飲茶。[ngoi5 hen4-dao2 ngim2-ca4]
We (will) have dim sum tomorrow.

今日係好日。[gim1-ngid5 hai3 hao2 ngid52]
Today is a good day.

你晏晝吃乜？[nei1 an1-jiu5 hieg1 mod2?]
What are you eating in the afternoon?

昨晚係禮拜二。[dam5-man52 hai3 lai5-bai1-ngei3]
Yesterday was Tuesday.

今日係禮拜日，唔係禮拜一。
[gim1-ngid5 hai3 lai5-bai1-ngid52, m4 hai3 lai5-bai1-yid2]
Today is Sunday, not Monday.

Recognizing Chinese Characters

一 [yid2] = one
天 [hen1/hen4] = sky; god
早 [dao2] = early; morning

Sample Conversation

Amy: 婆婆，今日係禮拜幾？
[puo4-puo42, gim1-ngid5 hai3 lai5-bai1 gei2?]
Popo, what day of the week is today?

Grandma: 我唔a隨。 [ngoi1 m4 ei1-tui4]
I don't know.

Amy: 今日係禮拜一。
[gim1-ngid5 hai3 lai5-bai1-yid2]
Today is Monday.

Grandma: 今日係禮拜一。
[gim1-ngid5 hai3 lai5-bai1-yid2]
Today is Monday.

Amy: 係，天早係禮拜二。
[hai3, hen4-dao2 hai3 lai5-bai1-ngei3]
Yes, (and) tomorrow is Tuesday.

Grandma: 哦。 [o5]
Okay.

1594。[yid2-ng2-giu2-lhei1]
1594.

Grandma

Amy

嘩，婆婆，你好犀利嘩！
[va3, puo4-puo42, nei1 hao2 sai1-lei3 va1]
Wow, grandma, you are awesome!

吽女。
[ngeu3-nui2]
Silly girl.

Grandma

See answers on page #117

Chapter 4 Exercises

1. What word do you add before a cardinal number to make it a day of the week?
   _____

2. How do you say, "On the weekends I like to ..."?
   _____

3. What does, "我嘅號碼係… (ngoi1 ge1 hao3-ma52 hai3 ...)" imply?
   _____

4. Do you conjugate the verb "係 (hai3) to be"?
   _____

5. Transliterate or translate the following sentences:

   今日係禮拜日。[gim1-ngid5 hai3 lai5-bai1-ngid52]
   _____

   天早係禮拜幾? [_____ _____ _____ _____ _____ _____?]
   What day of the week is tomorrow?

   我嘅號碼係 838-274-1710.
   [ngoi1 ge1 hao3-ma52 hai3 bad1-lham1-bad1, ngei3-tid2-lhei1, yid2-tid2-yid2-lieng4]
   _____

   My number is 831-092-6132.
   _____

A beginner's guide to mastering conversational Taishanese

Chapter 5

My Chinese Zodiac Sign is …

我屬 …

(ngoi1 sug3 …)

After learning the basic numbers in Taishanese, you can build on them to tell others more about yourself – your age, birthday, and zodiac sign. In this chapter, Grandma and I flip through her fortune telling calendar to practice saying dates, zodiac signs, and birthdays. After reading this chapter, you will be able to do the same by freely using numbers from 11 to 100 in Taishanese. You will see that once you learn the basics, conversing in Taishanese is not as hard as everyone thinks.

Now, let's review numbers from 0 to 10 in Taishanese.

In a fortune telling calendar, you can find an overwhelming amount of information, such as both the lunar and Gregorian dates, the zodiac signs that will have a good or bad day, and a list of actions that bring either good or bad luck for the day. Fortune telling calendars are more popular among the older generation.

零 [lieng4] 0

一 [yid2] 1

二 [ngei3] 2

三 [lham1] 3

四 [lhei1] 4

五 [ng2] 5

六 [lug3] 6

七 [tid2] 7

八 [bad1] 8

九 [giu2] 9

十 [sib3] 10

十六日 = the 16th day of the month in the lunar calendar

Vocabulary A

10 [sib3] + 1 [yid2] = 11 [sib3-yid2]
10 [sib3] + 5 [ng2] = 15 [sib3-ng2]

2 [ngei3] x 10 [sib3] = 20 [ngei3-sib3]

2 [ngei3] x 10 [sib3] + 7 [tid2] = 27 [ngei3-sib3-tid2]

4 [lhei1] x 10 [sib3] + 5 [ng2] = 45 [lhei1-sib3-ng2]

9 [giu2] x 10 [sib3] + 9 [giu2] = 99 [giu2-sib3-giu2]

Now, let's incorporate the numbers to tell others your age.

歲 [lhui1] = year (of age)

number + 歲 [lhui1] = ... years old*

我 [ngoi1] + 30 [lham1-sib3] + 歲 [lhui1] = I am 30 years old.

Note that 歲 (lhui1) can only be used for people, animals, or other animated objects such as cartoon characters like Hello Kitty and Pokemon.

Sample Sentences A

我7歲。 [ngoi1 tid2 lhui1]
I am seven years old.

你16歲。 [nei1 sib3-lug3 lhui1]
You are sixteen years old.

佢25歲。 [kui1 ngei3-sib3-ng2 lhui1]
He's twenty-five years old.

你幾歲啊? [nei1 gei2 lhui1 a1?]
How old are you?

偓婆婆86歲。 [ngoi5 puo4-puo42 bad1-sib3-lug3 lhui1]
My (maternal) grandma is 86 years old.

Fun Fact

If you talk about zodiac signs in a conversation, you can learn a lot about someone's age. There are twelve Chinese zodiac signs that correspond to a twelve-year cycle. If a person's zodiac sign is the ox, for example, you know they must have been born in either the year 1985, 1997, 2009, or, 2021. However, there can be exceptions, especially if your birthday is in either January or February, since the Chinese zodiac year follows the lunar calendar rather than the Gregorian calendar we typically use now. To make sure that you know your correct zodiac sign, use an online resource to convert your birthday to your Chinese zodiac sign.

偌婆婆幾歲啊? [nieg5 puo4-puo42 gei2 lhui1 a1?]
How old is your (maternal) grandma?

Now, let's take a look at what the twelve Chinese zodiac signs are.

Vocabulary B 🔊

鼠 [si2] = rat
牛 [ngeu4] = ox
虎 [fu2] = tiger
兔 [hu1] = rabbit
龍 [lung4] = dragon
蛇 [sie4] = snake
馬 [ma5] = horse
羊 [yieng4] = goat
猴 [heu4] = monkey
雞 [gai1] = rooster
狗 [geu2] = dog
豬 [ji1] = pig

RAT *si2* 鼠	OX *ngeu4* 牛	TIGER *fu2* 虎	RABBIT *hu1* 兔	DRAGON *lung4* 龍	SNAKE *sie4* 蛇	HORSE *ma5* 馬	GOAT *yieng4* 羊	MONKEY *heu4* 猴	ROOSTER *gai1* 雞	DOG *geu2* 狗	PIG *ji1* 豬
2020	2021	2022	2023	2024	2025	2026	2027	2028	2029	2030	2031
2008	2009	2010	2011	2012	2013	2014	2015	2016	2017	2018	2019
1996	1997	1998	1999	2000	2001	2002	2003	2004	2005	2006	2007
1984	1985	1986	1987	1988	1989	1990	1991	1992	1993	1994	1995
1972	1973	1974	1975	1976	1977	1978	1979	1980	1981	1982	1983
1960	1961	1962	1963	1964	1965	1966	1967	1968	1969	1970	1971
1948	1949	1950	1951	1952	1953	1954	1955	1956	1957	1958	1959
1936	1937	1938	1939	1940	1941	1942	1943	1944	1945	1946	1947
1924	1925	1926	1927	1928	1929	1930	1931	1932	1933	1934	1935
1912	1913	1914	1915	1916	1917	1918	1919	1920	1921	1922	1923
1900	1901	1902	1903	1904	1905	1906	1907	1908	1909	1910	1911

屬 [sug3] = to be classified as; to be part of

我 [ngoi1] + 屬 [sug3] + zodiac sign = My zodiac sign is …

我 [ngoi1] + 屬 [sug3] + 羊 [yieng4] = My Chinese zodiac sign is (a) goat.
(Word-for-word translation: I am classified as a goat.)

Sample Sentences B 🔊

我屬羊。[ngoi1 sug3 yieng4]
My Chinese zodiac sign is (a) goat.

佢屬馬。[kui1 sug3 ma5]
His/her zodiac sign is (a) horse.

倷爸屬雞? [nieg5 ba2 sug3 gai12?]
Your dad's zodiac sign is (a) rooster?

你屬乜? [nei1 sug3 mod2?]
What is your Chinese zodiac sign?

Note that all of these sentences use "屬 (sug3) to be classified as" instead of the verb "係 (hai3) to be." A common mistake that non-native speakers might make when mentioning their zodiac sign is saying "我係... (ngoi1 hai3) I am ..." However, you should not use the "我係... (ngoi1 hai3) I am ..." structure to indicate your zodiac sign because comparing a person to an animal can be degrading. For example, saying "我係豬 (ngoi1 hai3 ji1) I am a pig" would imply that you exhibit the undesirable traits of a pig such as being indolent and unintelligent.

Now, let's take a look at how to say an exact date in Chinese.

Vocabulary C 🔊

年 [nen4(2)] = year
月 [ngud3/ngud5] = month
日 [ngid3/ngid5(2)] = day
號 [hao3] = ...th day

A beginner's guide to mastering conversational Taishanese

2009年 [ngei3-lieng4-lieng4-giu2 nen42] = the year 2009
2010年 [ngei3-lieng4-yid2-lieng4 nen42] = the year 2010
2021年 [ngei3-lieng4-ngei3-yid2 nen42] = the year 2021

2021年7月18號 [ngei3-lieng4-ngei3-yid2 nen42 tid2-ngud3 sib3-bad1 hao3] = July 18th, 2021

2018年12月29號 [ngei3-lieng4-yid2-bad1 nen42 sib3-ngei3-ngud3 ngei3-sib3-giu2 hao3] = December 29th, 2018

> **Question: Why isn't the year placed at the end of the date?**
>
> That is due to a cross-cultural difference between Asian countries and Western countries. Chinese culture considers a whole before its parts, and therefore often emphasizes the big over the small. For example, when Chinese people refer to a date, they go from the year to the month, and then to the day. When they mention an address, they go from the state to the city, and from the street to the house number. As you might have heard, Chinese speakers also say their last name before their first name. Just remember that bigger units always come before smaller units.

Sample Sentences C

今日係1月8號。[gim1-ngid5 hai3 yid2-ngud3 bad1 hao3]
Today is January 8th.

偓媽嘅生日係4月28號。[ngoi5 ma2 ge1 sang1-ngid3 hai3 lhei1-ngud3 ngei3-sib3-bad1 hao3]
My mom's birthday is on April 28th.

2021年係好年。[ngei3-lieng4-ngei3-yid2 nen42 hai3 hao2 nen42]
(Year) 2021 was a good year.

偓人嘅生日係7月19號。[nieg5 ngin4 ge1 sang1-ngid3 hai3 tid2-ngud3 sib3-giu2 hao3]
Your paternal grandma's birthday is on July 19th.

偓人嘅生日係幾時？[nieg5 ngin4 ge1 sang1-ngid3 hai3 gei2-si52?]
When is your (paternal) grandma's birthday?

今日係幾月幾號啊？[gim1-ngid5 hai3 gei2 ngud3 gei2 hao3 a1?]
What is today's date? (Word-for-word translation: Today is what month and what number?)

Recognizing Chinese Characters

牛 [ngeu4] = ox, cow
年 [nen4(2)] = year
月 [ngud3/ngud5] = month

Sample Conversation

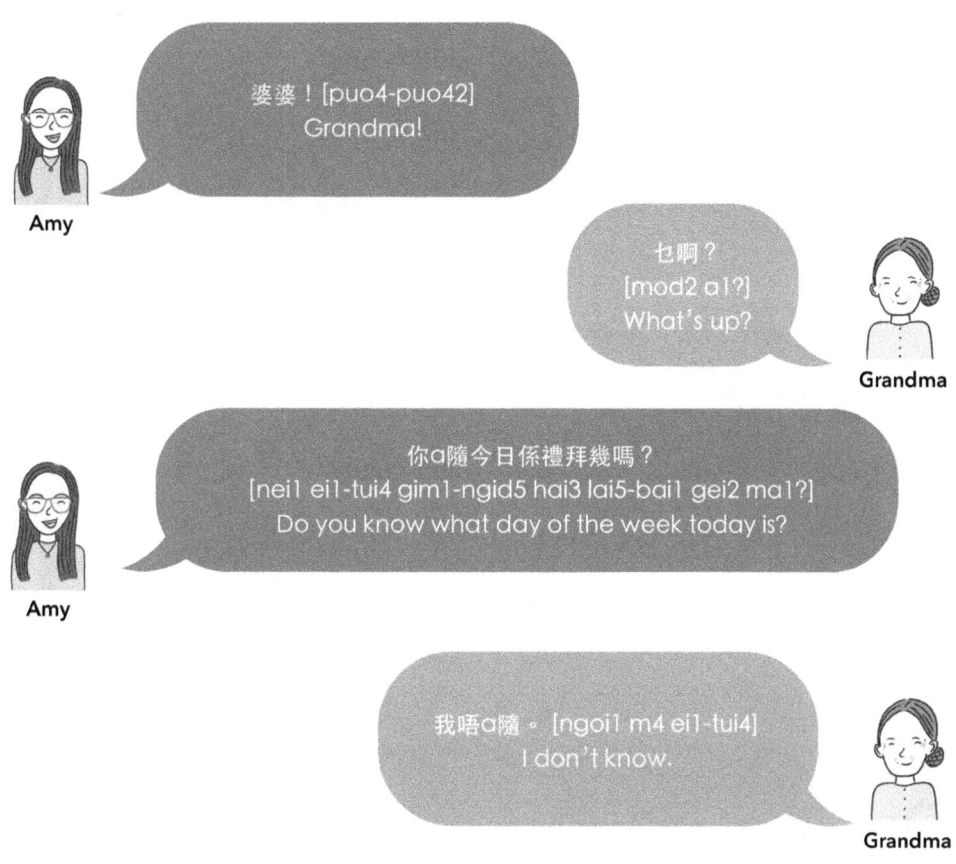

Amy: 我同你去睇日曆。
[ngoi1 hung4 nei1 hui1 hai2 ngid3-led3]
I (will) go look at the calendar with you.

Grandma: 哦。[o5]
Okay.

Amy: 今日係禮拜一。
[gim1-ngid5 hai3 lai5-bai1-yid2]
Today is Monday.

Grandma: 嘩，今日係幾月幾號啊？
[va3, gim1-ngid5 hai3 gei2 ngud3 gei2 hao3 a1?]
Wow, what is the date today?

Amy: 今日係7月15號。
[gim1-ngid5 hai3 tid2-ngud3 sib3-ng2 hao3]
Today is July 15th.

Grandma: 哦。[o5]
Oh.

Amy: 我嘅生日係7月20號。
[ngoi1 ge1 sang1-ngid3 hai3 tid2-ngud3 ngei3-sib3 hao3]
My birthday is on July 20th.

Learn to Speak Taishanese 1

Grandma

嘩，你屬乜啊？
[va3, nei1 sug3 mod2 a1?]
Wow, what is your Chinese zodiac sign?

Amy

我屬豬。你呢？
[ngoi1 sug3 ji1, nei1 ne2?]
My zodiac sign is (a) pig. What about you?

Grandma

該個我a隨。我屬龍。
[koi5-goi1 ngoi1 ei1-tui4. ngoi1 sug3 lung4]
This I know. My zodiac sign is (a) dragon.

Amy

係啊，你好叻啊，婆婆！
[hai3 a1, nei1 hao2 lieg2 a1, puo4-puo42!]
Yes, you are so smart, Grandma!

A beginner's guide to mastering conversational Taishanese

Cultural Insights | Traditional Chinese Banquets

Traditional Chinese banquets are generally held for weddings "喜酒 (hei2-diu2)", a child's one-month old celebration "滿月酒 (mon2-ngud5-diu2)" (similar to a baby shower but it happens after the baby's birth), and an elderly person's 60th, 70th or 80th birthday "大壽 (ai3-siu3)." The size, formality, and distinction of the banquet depends on the budget of the host, and each table can usually fit 10 to 12 people. In the U.S., friends and families will usually return the host's generosity by giving wedding or baby gifts from registries. In a traditional Chinese banquet, it is very common for guests to give cash by putting it in a red envelope and handing it to the host while saying a couple of blessing words in Chinese.

紅 [hung4] = red
包 [bao1] = bag

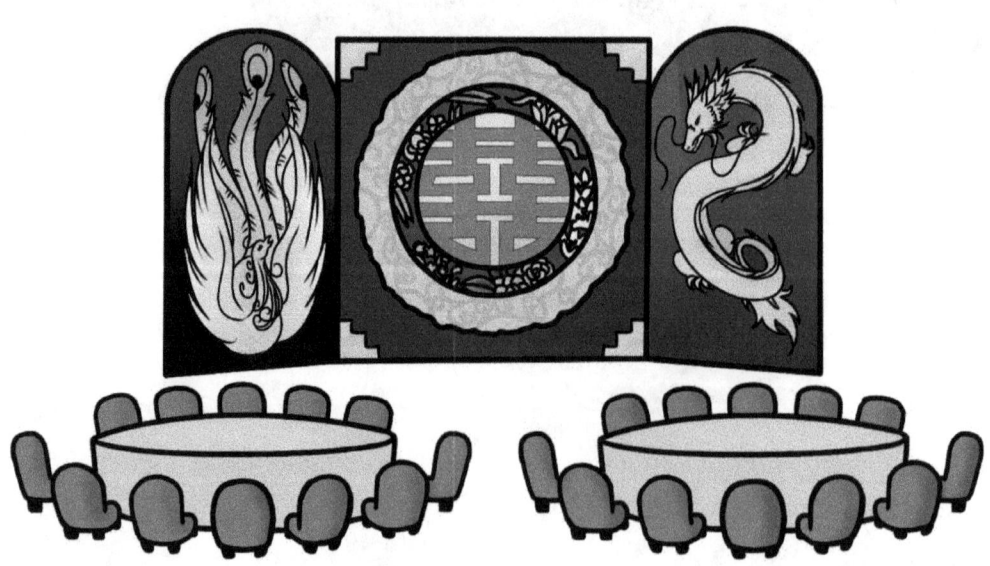

Chapter 5 Exercises

1. What is the order of words when expressing a date in Chinese?

   _____

2. Can you use 歲 (lhui1) to express the age of a building?

   _____

3. Translate or transliterate the following sentences:

   When is your birthday?

   _____

   My birthday is June 14th.

   _____

   [gim1-ngid5 hai3 ngei3-lieng4-ngei3-lhei1 nen42 giu2-ngud3 sib3-lug3-hao3]
   今日係2024年9月16號。

   _____

4. Fill in the blanks.

   我45歲。[ngoi1_____ _____ _____ lhui1]
   I am forty-five years old.

   今日係我生日。[_____ _____ hai3 ngoi1 sang1-ngid3]
   Today is my birthday.

Chapter 6

I don't feel well
我唔舒服
(ngoi1 m4 si1-fug3)

Part of the reason why I decided to move back to Chinatown and stay with Popo was to take care of her and be a translator whenever she needs me. For an Alzheimer's patient, it is difficult to not only express thoughts and feelings, but also levels of pain and descriptions of discomfort. In Chapter 6, I patiently ask Grandma where she is not feeling well and help translate what she said to the doctor.

After reading this chapter, you will be able to distinguish body parts and express the severity of your symptoms and discomfort in Taishanese.

Now, let's take a look at the body parts in Taishanese.

Vocabulary A 🔊

手 [siu2] = hand
腳 [gieg1] = foot
面 [men3] = face
眼 [ngan2] = eye
頭 [heu4] = head
口 [heu2] = mouth
鼻 [bei3] = nose
耳 [ngei2] = ear
肚 [u2] = belly; stomach
頸喉 [gieng2-heu5] = throat

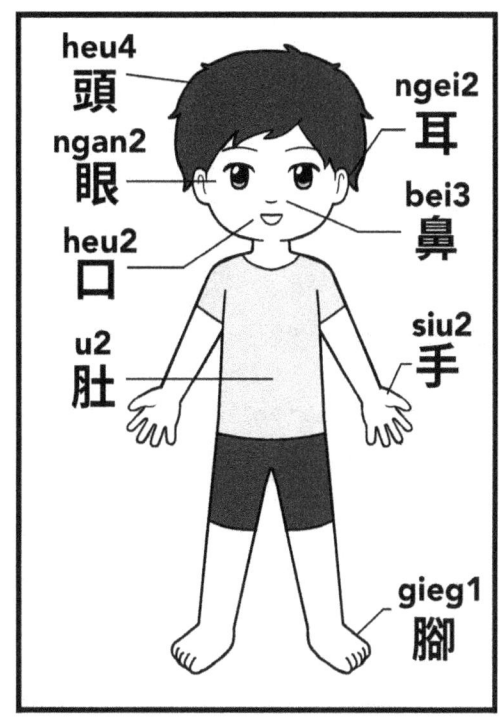

Sample Sentences A 🔊

該個係鼻。[koi5-goi1 hai3 bei3]
This is the nose.

你嘅眼好大。[nei1 ge1 ngan2 hao2 ai3]
Your eyes are very big.

你嘅耳仔到乃啊?[nei1 ge1 ngei2-doi2 ao1 nai52 a1?]
Where are your little ears?

Using 仔 (doi2) after a noun adds informality and intimacy to the tone of the sentence, for example, "your ears" vs. "your little ears."

我嘅腳赤。[ngoi1 ge1 gieg1 tieg1]
My foot hurts.   　　　　| 赤 [tieg1] = pain

你乃赤?[nei1 nai52 tieg1?]
Where are you hurting?

你嘅手赤?[nei1 ge1 siu2 tieg12?]
Your hand hurts?

A beginner's guide to mastering conversational Taishanese

你嘅手赤嗎? [nei1 ge1 siu2 tieg1 ma1?]
Does your hand hurt?

Now, let's learn more about ways to describe symptoms in Taishanese by using the body part terms we have just learned.

舒服 [si1-fug3] = to be comfortable
唔舒服 [m4 si1-fug3] = to be uncomfortable; to be sick

Vocabulary B 🔊

頭赤 [heu4 tieg1] = headache
肚赤 [u2 tieg1] = stomachache
頸喉赤 [gieng2-heu5 tieg1] = to have a sore throat
感冒 [gam2-mao3] = to catch a cold
咳 [kad2] = to cough
發燒 [fad1-sieu1] = to have a fever
飆屎 [bieu1-si2] = to have diarrhea

Sample Sentences B 🔊

我唔舒服。[ngoi1 m4 si1-fug3]
I don't feel well.

你係唔係唔舒服? [nei1 hai3 m4 hai3 m4 si1-fug3?]
Are you not feeling well?

你乃唔舒服? [nei1 nai52 m4 si1-fug3?]
Where are you not feeling well?

我發燒。[ngoi1 fad1-sieu1]
I have a fever.

佢頸喉赤。[kui1 gieng2-heu5 tieg1]
He/she has a sore throat.

你今日肚赤? [nei1 gim1-ngid5 u2 tieg12?]
You have a stomachache today?

Now that you have learned how to describe symptoms in Taishanese, let's learn some commonly used terms at the doctor's office.

Vocabulary C 🔊

打針 [a1 jim52] = to have a shot
打疫苗 [a2 ved3-mieu4] = to get a vaccine
心跳 [lhim1-hieu1] = heartbeat
體重 [hai2-cung12] = body weight
血壓 [hud2-ad2] = blood pressure
量血壓 [lieng4 hud2-ad2] = to measure blood pressure

血壓高 [hud2-ad2 gao1] = high blood pressure
血壓低 [hud2-ad2 ai1] = low blood pressure

Sample Sentences C 🔊

婆婆要打針。[puo4-puo42 yieu1 a2-jim52]
Popo needs to have a shot.

你嘅血壓係幾多? [nei1 ge1 hud2-ad2 hai3 gei2-uo12?]
What is your blood pressure?

佢唔想打疫苗。[kui1 m4 lhieng2 a2 ved3-mieu4]
He/she doesn't want to get the vaccine.

爺爺量血壓。[yie4-yie42 lieng4 hud2-ad2]
Grandpa measures the (his) blood pressure.

唔該,乃量血壓啊? [m4-goi1, nai52 lieng4 hud2-ad2 a1?]
Excuse me, where can I have (my) blood pressure measured?

你要打針嗎? [nei1 yieu1 a2-jim52 ma1?]
Do you need a shot?

你有血壓高。 [nei1 yiu1 hud2-ad2 gao1]
You have high blood pressure.

Recognizing Chinese Characters

口 [heu2] = mouth
手 [siu2] = hand
肚 [u2] = stomach

Sample Conversation 🔊

Nurse

婆婆，你好。
[puo4-puo42, nei1-hao2]
Hi, popo*.

*Not only can the phrase "popo" be used to address your own maternal grandma, it can also be used to address any elderly woman, as you can see here.

Learn to Speak Taishanese 1

你好。
[nei1-hao2]
Hi.

Grandma

Nurse

我同你量血壓。
[ngoi1 hung4 nei1 lieng4 hud2-ad2]
I (will) measure the (your) blood pressure for you.

哦。[o5]
Okay.

Grandma

Nurse

你乃唔舒服？你頭赤？
[nei1 nai52 m4 si1-fug3? nei1 heu4 tieg12?]
Where do you not feel well? Are you having a headache?

唔係。
[m4 hai3]
No.

Grandma

Nurse

你感冒？[nei1 gam2-mao32?]
Are you having a cold?

偓婆婆肚赤。
[ngoi5 puo4-puo42 u2 tieg1]
My grandma has a stomachache.

Amy

A beginner's guide to mastering conversational Taishanese

Cultural Insights | What is 熱氣 (yeet-hay in Cantonese) / (nged3-hei1 in Taishanese) and what do you do when you are 熱氣 (nged3-hei1)?

Traditional Chinese Medicine, or TCM 中醫 (jung1-yi1), includes both herbs and health and wellness practices such as Qi Gong and acupuncture. There are over 300 herbs that are commonly prescribed in Chinese medicinal practice. The effectiveness of traditional Chinese medicine for treating different diseases is debatable, but the goal of using TCM is to keep or regain balance in your body. An extremely common diagnosis in TCM is 熱氣 (nged3-hei1), or sometimes romanized as yit-hei or yeet-hay in Cantonese. A very common symptom of 熱氣 (nged3-hei1) is a sore throat.

In TCM, 熱氣 (nged3-hei1), which literally means "hot air" in Chinese, refers to the yin-yang imbalance of a person caused by the hot properties of food. There are some foods, such as those that have hot properties, that trigger this imbalance because excess heat in the system damages the liver. Hot food includes red and black peppers, alcohol, and any deep-fried food, which are spicy, hot, and warming. On the other hand, cool food includes peppermint, which makes you feel cooled and refreshed.

Particular herbal tea mixes and soups are common remedies to treat 熱氣 (nged3-hei1). You can easily find herbal tea shops anywhere in Guangdong and Hong Kong. If you live overseas, you can also find these herbal teas in most Chinese bakeries and in packaged form in Chinese supermarkets.

See answers on page #117

Chapter 6 Exercises

1. What word do you use to tell someone that something is hurting?

   _____

2. How do you express, "I have a headache?"

   _____

3. How do you tell someone that you are not feeling well?

   _____

4. Label the following body parts in Taishanese.

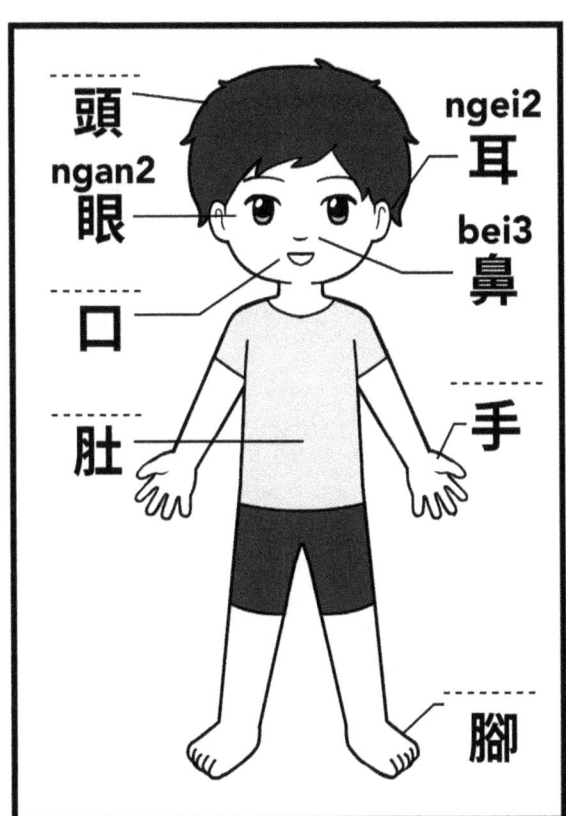

5. Translate the following sentences.

   佢發燒。[kui1 fad1-sieu1]

   _____

   我禮拜四打疫苗。[ngoi1 lai5-bai1-lhei1 a2 ved3-mieu4]

   _____

   你頸喉赤唔赤？[nei1 gieng2-heu5 tieg1 m4 tieg1?]

   _____

Part II Review

- To specify the days of the week, you add "禮拜 (lai5-bai1) week" before the cardinal number, except for Sunday, in which you add "日 (ngid52) sun".
- To tell someone your age, you can say, "我…歲 (ngoi1 … lhui1)," adding your age in between "ngoi1" and "lhui1."
- How old = 幾歲 (gei2 lhui1)
- When = 幾時 (gei2 si52)
- To tell someone your Chinese zodiac sign, you can say, "我屬 (ngoi1 sug3)… my Chinese zodiac sign is …."
- Month of the year = Number + 月 (ngud3)
- Day of the month = Number + 號 (hao3)
- Where = 乃 (nai52)
- To express discomfort that is caused by pain, you can say noun + 赤 (tieg1).
- To let someone know that you are not feeling well, you say, "我唔舒服 (ngoi1 m4 si1-fug3)".

Sample Paragraph

今日係禮拜三。我嘅生日係5月16號。我34歲，屬兔。我生日唔a隨做乜，好頭赤。
[gim1-ngid5 hai3 lai5-bai1-lham1. ngoi1 ge1 sang1-ngid3 hai3 ng2-ngud3 sib3-lug3 hao3. ngoi1 lham1-sib3-lhei1 lhui1, sug3 hu1. ngoi1 sang1-ngid3 m4 ei1-tui4 du1 mod2, hao2 heu4 tieg1]

English Translation:
Today is Wednesday. My birthday is on May 16th. I am 34 years old, (and my) Chinese zodiac sign is (a) rabbit. I don't know what to do on my birthday (and that is causing me) a headache.

Sample Exercises

Transliterate the following phrases.

July 25th [_____ _____ _____ _____ _____ _____]

See answers on page #118

Yesterday he had a headache. [____ ____ ____ ____ ____]

I don't know your zodiac sign. [____ ____ ____ ____ ____ ____ ____]

Chapter 7

Taking ... medicine
吃...藥
(hieg1 ... yieg5)

After seeing the doctor with Grandma, I picked up her prescription at a local pharmacy. I then explained the medication instructions to the home health aide.

In this chapter, you will learn some terms related to medication in Taishanese. You will learn how to give instructions on the frequency and amount of medicine needed. In addition, you will also learn some commonly used terms that will help your sick elders at home.

Now, let's take a look at some common medications.

Vocabulary A 🔊

藥 [yieg5] = medicine; medication
藥水 [yieg5-sui2] = liquid medication
感冒藥 [gam2-mao3 yieg5] = cold medication
咳藥 [kad2 yieg5] = cough medication
發燒藥 [fad1-sieu1 yieg5] = fever medication
肚赤藥 [u2-tieg1 yieg5] = stomachache medication

Sample Sentences A 🔊

咳藥到乃啊？[kad2 yieg5 ao1 nai52 a1?]
Where is the cough medication?

該尼係你嘅藥。[koi5-nai2 hai3 nei1 ge1 yieg5]
These are your medications.

該尼係婆婆嘅藥。[koi5-nai2 hai3 puo4-puo42 ge1 yieg5]
These are grandma's medications.

該尼係乜藥啊？[koi5-nai2 hai3 mod2 yieg5 a1?]
What medications are these?

嚀尼係感冒藥。[nen5-nai2 hai3 gam2-mao3 yieg5]
Those are cold medications.

嚀個藥水幾好！[nen5-goi1 yieg5-sui2 gei2 hao2!]
That liquid medication is quite good (effective)!

你要吃藥。[nei1 yieu1 hieg1 yieg5]
You have to take (the) medication.

我唔吃藥。[ngoi1 m4 hieg1 yieg5]
I am not taking (the) medication.

該尼 [koi5-nai2] = these
嚀尼 [nen5-nai2] = those

In Chinese, the verb for taking medication is 吃 (hieg1), to eat.

Now, let's add more details in order to give instructions for taking medication.

Vocabulary B 🔊

一 [yid2] = one
半 [bon1/bon5] = half
一日 [yid2-ngid1] = one day
一次 [yid2-lhu1] = one time
一粒 [yid2-lib1] = one capsule
一羹 [yid2-gang1] = one spoonful
一杯 [yid2-boi1] = one cup
一啖 [yid2-am3] = one sip

Sample Sentences B 🔊

一日吃三次。[yid2-ngid1 hieg1 lham1-lhu1]
Take it three times per day.

一次吃兩粒。[yid2-lhu1 hieg1 lieng2-lib1]
Take two capsules each time.

Question: Why do you say "兩粒 (lieng2-lib1)" instead of "二粒 (ngei3 -lib1)" for "two capsules"?

In Chinese, the number 2 is an exception to the rules. When you are trying to quantify something with the number 2, you always use "兩 (lieng2)." For example, when you are trying to say two units of something, such as "two cups of coffee," "two people," or even "two o'clock," you would say "兩 (lieng2)." However, when you are counting "1, 2, 3, 4, …," you would use "二 (ngei3)."

該杯藥水係你嘅。[koi5-boi1 yieg5-sui2 hai3 nei1 ge1]
This cup of liquid medication is yours.

你一日要吃三次感冒藥。[nei1 yid2-ngid1 yieu1 hieg1 lham1-lhu1 gam2-mao3 yieg5]
You have to take the cold medication three times per day.

佢吃一啖咳藥水。[kui1 hieg1 yid2-am3 kad2 yieg5-sui2]
He/she has one sip of liquid medication.

吃一羹, 好嗎? [hieg1 yid2-gang1, hao2 ma1?]
Take a spoonful (of it), please?

Vocabulary C 🔊

尿 [nieu3] = urine
屙尿 [uo1 nieu3] = to pee
屎 [si2] = stool
屙屎 [uo1 si2] = to poop
屁 [pei1] = fart
放屁 [fong1-pei1] = to fart
廁所 [lhu1-suo2] = bathroom
去廁所 [hui1 lhu1-suo2] = to go to the bathroom

Sample Sentences C 🔊

我要去廁所。[ngoi1 yieu1 hui1 lhu1-suo2]
I need to go to the bathroom.

你想去廁所? [nei1 lhieng2 hui1 lhu1-suo2?]
You want to go to the bathroom?

爺爺, 你要去廁所? [yie4-yie42, nei1 yieu1 hui1 lhu1-suo2?]
Grandpa, (do) you need to go to the bathroom?

佢去廁所屙尿。[kui1 hui1 lhu1-suo2 uo1 nieu3]
He/she is going to the bathroom to pee.

BB要屙屎嘩! [bi4-bi2 yieu1 uo1 si2 va1!]
The baby has to poop!

Recognizing Chinese Characters

藥 [yieg5] = medicine
次 [lhu1] = (one) time
杯 [boi1] = cup

Sample Conversation 🔊

Home aide

婆婆幾浩啊？
[puo4-puo42 gei2-hao52 a1?]
How is Popo?

醫生有開藥。
[yi1-sang12 yiu1 hoi1-yieg5]
The doctor prescribed (some) medication.

Amy

Home aide

乜藥啊？
[mod2 yieg5 a1?]
What kind of medication?

肚赤藥。婆婆一日要吃三次，一次要吃一粒。
[u2-tieg1 yieg5. puo4-puo42 yid2-ngid1 yieu1 hieg1 lham1-lhu1, yid2-lhu1 yieu1 hieg1 yid2-lib1]
Medication for her stomachache. Popo has to take it three times a day, (and) one capsule each time.

Amy

佢吃藥前要吃嘢。
[kui1 hieg1 yieg5 ten4 yieu1 hieg1 yie1]
She has to eat something before she takes the medication.

Home aide

有冇藥水啊？ [yiu1 mao1 yieg5-sui2 a1?]
Is there any liquid medication?

冇。唔該你照顧婆婆！
[mao1. m4-goi1 nei1 jieu1-gu1 puo4-puo42!]
No. Thank you for taking care of Grandma!

Amy

Cultural Insights | What You Should Expect In Chinese Households

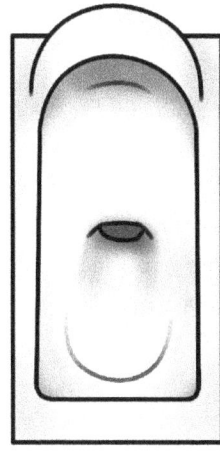

This is what a squat toilet looks like

This is how you use a squat toilet

When you are visiting the home of a Chinese family or relative, always ask if it's necessary to take off your shoes and switch to a pair of slippers, because it is a Chinese custom to remove shoes at the door. It is always better to ask to show politeness even if the host says no.

One of the reasons why slippers are preferred in a household is to prevent dust and dirt from entering the home. In addition, most places (households and even public spaces) in China have squat toilets. Therefore, slippers will help to keep both the home and your feet clean.

When seated toilets were first introduced in Taishan and the rest of mainland China in the 1980s, it was a sign of modernity and luxury that you could only find in upscale restaurants and households. Seated toilets gained popularity after the 1990s and, in modern times, it is not rare to find a seated toilet in a household in Taishan. However, squat toilets are still the norm for public bathrooms.

What are some pros and cons of squat toilets?

When people use squat toilets, it is easier to poop because squatting helps to empty the bowels more completely while straining less. Using a squat toilet is also beneficial for easing constipation and hemorrhoids (imagine practicing yoga squats every time you have to use the toilet). In addition to these health benefits, it is also considered more hygienic for individuals in public bathrooms due to the lack of direct contact with one's skin, serving a similar purpose as toilet seat covers in Western countries. As a bonus, if you have pets, it is much easier to train them to use a squat toilet. Not only can you keep the house clean, but it is also more convenient for your pet to use the toilet at any time without supervision.

Although squat toilets are popular in many Asian countries, it is very difficult for Westerners to imagine using them daily. The first concern comes from the awkward posture, and many people with weak knees might not be able to squat for such a long time without feeling numb. It is especially unpleasant for those who experience constipation. The second issue is that people conceive of squat toilets as being very dirty. However, the cleanliness of public bathrooms might involve other underlying variables, such as the fact that squat toilets are usually built in less developed regions with less resources to hire cleaning staff.

It is easy for people from one culture to think their practices are superior to others' when making snap judgments. But when we look at these differences with curiosity rather than judgment, we will often find something fascinating. For example, although squat toilets are still widely labeled as inferior in Western countries, they are now becoming more trendy due to their health benefits.

Chapter 7 Exercises

1. What is the general verb used to describe taking medication?

   _____

2. What is the verb used when taking a liquid medication?

   _____

3. What is the classifier for "one capsule"?

   _____

4. How do you tell someone the frequency of medicine intake per day?

   _____

5. Translate and transliterate the following sentences.

   [nei1 hieg1 kad2 yieg5]
   你吃咳藥。

   _____

   [kui1 yid2-ngid1 hieg1 lham1-lhu1 yieg5]
   佢一日吃三次藥。

   _____

   Take four capsules each time.

   _____

6. Connect the Chinese vocabulary with their appropriate translations.

發燒藥 [fad1-sieu1 yieg5]   cough medication

感冒藥 [gam2-mao3 yieg5]   liquid medication

肚赤藥 [u2-tieg1 yieg5]   cold medication

咳藥 [kad2 yieg5]   fever medication

藥水 [yieg5-sui2]   stomachache medication

Chapter 8

I am in …
我到…
(ngoi1 ao1 …)

As you might already be able to tell, Grandma's home aide has been taking great care of Popo. She makes Grandma feel comfortable with her attentive care, hard work, and use of Taishanese.

In this chapter, I have a conversation with the home aide to get to know her better by asking about where she lives and her commute. After reading this chapter, you will be able to tell someone your location, a mode of transportation, and how to get from one place to another.

A beginner's guide to mastering conversational Taishanese

Vocabulary A 🔊

工 [gung1] = work
做工 [du1-gung1] = to work; to do work
返工 [fan1-gung1] = to go to work
返學 [fan1-hog3] = to go to school

地鐵 [ei3-hed1] = subway
巴士 [ba2-si52] = bus
的士 [ded2-si52] = taxi

行路 [hang4-lu3] = to walk
搭 [ab1] = to ride; to take (a vehicle)
車 [cie1] = to drive (a car)
搭車 [ab1 cie1] = to ride a car; to take a bus/subway

Sample Sentences A 🔊

我行路。[ngoi1 hang4-lu3]
I walk.

我開車返工。[ngoi1 hoi1 cie1 fan1-gung1]
I drive to go to work.

我搭地鐵返工。[ngoi1 ab1 ei3-hed1 fan1-gung1]
I take the subway to go to work.

我搭D車返工。[ngoi1 ab1 di2 cie1 fan1-gung1]
I take the D train to go to work.

你搭N車返學?[nei1 ab1 en2 cie1 fan1-hog32?]
You take the N train to go to school?

Now let's learn how to tell someone your location.

Vocabulary B 🔊

美國 [mei5-gog2] = the United States

加拿大 [ga1-na4-ai32] = Canada

紐約 [niu2-yieg2] = New York

加州 [ga1-jiu1] = California

三藩市 [lham1-fan4-si52] = San Francisco

多倫多 [uo1-lun4-uo1] = Toronto

溫哥華 [vun1-guo2-va4] = Vancouver

乃 [nai52] = where

大道 [ai3-ao3] = avenue

街 [gai5(2)] = street

唐人街 [hong4-ngin4-gai5] = Chinatown

到 [ao1] = at; in

我到…做工。 [ngoi1 ao1 … du1-gung1] = I work in …

我到…住。 [ngoi1 ao1 … ji3] = I live in …

> Remember, the most basic sentence structure in Chinese is subject-verb-object. So a handy tip for forming a Chinese sentence is to place your main verb phrase at the end of your sentence.

A quick review of Taishanese numbers

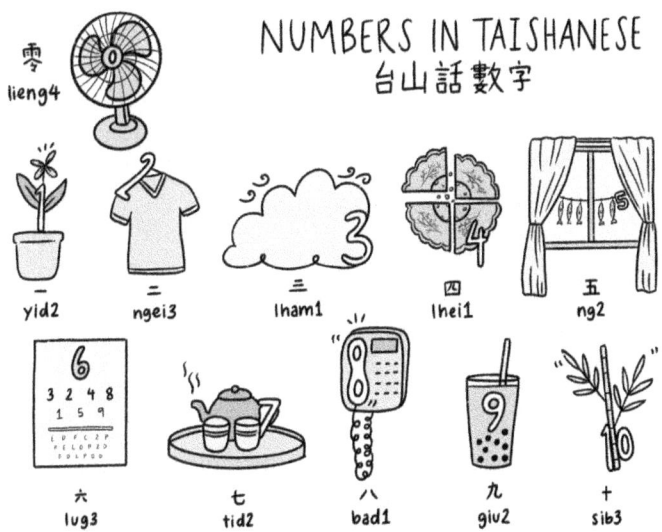

A beginner's guide to mastering conversational Taishanese

Now, let's take a look at how to use these terms in sentences.

Sample Sentences B 🔊

我到唐人街做工。 [ngoi1 ao1 hong4-ngin4-gai5 du1-gung1]
I work in Chinatown.

我到14街做工。 [ngoi1 ao1 sib3-lhei1 gai52 du1-gung1]
I work on 14th Street.

你到22街做工，係唔係啊? [nei1 ao1 ngei3-sib3-ngei3 gai52 du1-gung1, hai3-m4-hai3 a1?]
You work on 22nd Street. Is that true?

佢到13大道83街住。 [kui1 ao1 sib3-lham1 ai3-ao3 bad1-sib3-lham1 gai52 ji3]
He/she lives on 13th Avenue and 83rd Street.

你有冇屋企人到紐約? [nei1 yiu1-mao1 ug2-kei2 ngin4 ao1 niu2-yieg2?]
Do you have any family members in New York?

我有屋企人到加州。 [ngoi1 yiu1 ug2-kei2 ngin4 ao1 ga1-jiu1]
I have family members in California.

Vocabulary C

頭先 [heu4-lhen12] = before; just now

該時 [koi5-si52] = now

一陣 [yid2-jin52] = later

Sample Sentences C 🔊

你頭先到乃? [nei1 heu4-lhen12 ao1 nai52?]
Where were you before?

頭先偓妹返學。[heu4-lhen12 ngoi5 moi5 fan1-hog3]
My younger sister just (left to) go to school.

你該時到乃？[nei1 koi5-si52 ao1 nai52?]
Where are you now?

我唔a隨我該時到乃。[ngoi1 m4 ei1-tui4 ngoi1 koi5-si52 ao1 nai52]
I don't know where I am right now.

偓人人一陣去34街。[ngoi5 ngin4-ngin4 yid2-jin52 hui1 lham1-sib3-lhei1 gai52]
My (paternal) grandma will go to 34th Street later.

Recognizing Chinese Characters

大 [ai3] = big
道 [ao3] = path
街 [gai5(2)] = street

Sample Conversation

阿姨，你幾浩返工啊？
[a1 yi2, nei1 gei2-hao52 fan1-gung1 a1?]
Auntie*, how do you come to work?

Amy

Home aide

我搭地鐵返工。
[ngoi1 ab1 ei3-hed1 fan1-gung1]
I take the subway to come to work.

*In Chinese, you often call a lady who is around your mother's age 阿姨 (a1 yi2), auntie, and a man who is around your dad's age 阿叔 (a1 sug2), uncle.

你搭乜車啊？
[nei1 ab1 mod2 cie1 a1?]
Which train do you take?

Amy

Home aide

我搭N車返工。
[ngoi1 ab1 en2 cie1 fan1-gung1]
I take the N train to come to work.

你到乃住啊？
[nei1 ao1 nai52 ji3 a1?]
Where do you live?

Amy

Home aide

跑華街。
[pao2-va4 gai5]
Powell Street.

哦。你一陣去乃啊，阿姨？
[o5. nei1 yid2-jin52 hui1 nai52 a1, a1 yi2?]
Oh I see. Where are you going later, auntie?

Amy

Home aide

我一陣返屋企。
[ngoi1 yid2-jin52 fan1 ug2-kei2]
I am going home later.

Cultural Insights | Why is Chinatown called "唐人街 (hong4-ngin4-gai5)?"

Chinatown 唐人街 (hong4-ngin4-gai5) means the street of 唐人 (hong4-ngin4), or Chinese people. The 唐 (hong4) in 唐人 (hong4-ngin4) refers to the Tang Dynasty, which was one of the most prosperous and successful dynasties throughout Chinese history, from foreign affairs to internal governance. Therefore, the Chinese diaspora calls itself 唐人 (hong4-ngin4), which literally means "people of Tang."

Besides 唐人街 (hong4-ngin4-gai5), Chinatown can also be called 華埠 (va4-feu3) in Taishanese and Cantonese communities. 華 (va4) represents Chinese, and 埠 (feu3) represents a city, state, port and pier. 唐人 (hong4-ngin4) and 華人 (va4-ngin4) are two popular ways to address "Chinese people" other than 中國人 (jung1-gog2 ngin4), which literally translates to "China people".

Chapter 8 Exercises

1. What is the Taishanese preposition equivalent to "at" in English?

   _____

2. How would you ask someone where he/she lives?

   _____

3. How do you say "Chinatown" in Taishanese?

   _____

4. Translate or transliterate the following sentences:

   我頭先返工。[ngoi1 heu4-lhen12 fan1-gung1]

   _____

   我搭B車返學。[ngoi1 ab1 bi2 cie1 fan1-hog3]

   _____

   你到乃返工？[nei1 ao1 nai52 fan1-gung1?]

   _____

5. Fill in the blanks.

   A: How do you go to work?

   B: 我搭Q車返工。[ngoi1 _____ kiu2 _____ fan1-gung1]

Chapter 9

How much is …?

…幾錢?

(… gei2-ten42?)

In Chapter 9, I am in a local Chinese bakery to order a bubble tea for myself and a coffee for Grandma. Many Alzheimer's patients often feel lethargic and lose their sense of time. This is the case for Grandma as well. To prevent her from sleeping too much during the day, I sometimes bring her a coffee and some of her favorite pastries from the Chinese bakery.

After reading this chapter, you will be able to order a beverage at your favorite Chinese bakery and understand how much your order costs. In Chapter 2, we learned that the simplest way to order is by saying, "I would like to have 我想攞 (ngoi1 lhieng2 huo2) …." In this chapter, we will further explore how to make a more detailed order.

A beginner's guide to mastering conversational Taishanese

杯 [boi1] = cup; glass (as a container)
一杯 [yid2-boi1] = one cup of

Remember the generic classifier we learned in Chapter 3? 個 (goi1) is a generic classifier for items.

Vocabulary A 🔊

大 [ai3] = big; large
中 [jung1] = medium
細 [lhai1] = small
細杯 [lhai1 boi1] = small cup of …
咖啡 [ga1-fie2] = coffee

一杯 [yid2-boi1] + 大杯 [ai3 boi1] + 咖啡 [ga1-fie2] = a large (cup of) coffee

Sample Sentences A 🔊

我想攞一杯大杯咖啡。
[ngoi1 lhieng2 huo2 yid2-boi1 ai3 boi1 ga1-fie2]
I would like a large (cup of) coffee.

我想攞兩杯中杯咖啡。
[ngoi1 lhieng2 huo2 lieng2-boi1 jung1 boi1 ga1-fie2]
I would like two medium (cups of) coffee.

我想攞三杯細杯咖啡。
[ngoi1 lhieng2 huo2 lham1-boi1 lhai1 boi1 ga1-fie2]
I would like three small (cups of) coffee.

As a reminder, in Chapter 7, we learned that 兩 (lieng2) is used as "two" when you are quantifying something.

Do you remember the definition of 攞 (huo2) from Chapter 2?

攞 [huo2] = to get
唔 [m4] = not

唔 [m4] + 攞 [huo2] = to not get; to not want
糖 [hong4] = sugar
唔攞 [m4 huo2] + 糖 [hong4] = to not want sugar

Vocabulary B 🔊

奶 [nai5] = milk
茶 [ca4] = tea
奶茶 [nai5-ca4] = milk tea
珍珠 [jin1-ji1] = pearl
珍珠奶茶 [jin1-ji1 nai5-ca4] = bubble tea

Sample Sentences B 🔊

我想攞一杯奶茶, 唔攞糖。
[ngoi1 lhieng2 huo2 yid2-boi1 nai5-ca4, m4 huo2 hong4]
I would like a (cup of) milk tea, (and) I don't want sugar.

我想攞一杯咖啡, 唔攞糖, 攞奶。
[ngoi1 lhieng2 huo2 yid2-boi1 ga1-fie2, m4 huo2 hong4, huo2 nai5]
I would like a (cup of) coffee; I don't want sugar (and) I want milk.

我想攞一杯咖啡, 攞少糖, 多奶。
[ngoi1 lhieng2 huo2 yid2-boi1 ga1-fie2, huo2 sieu2 hong4, uo1 nai5]
I would like a (cup of) coffee; I want less sugar (and) more milk.

| 少 [sieu2] = little | 多 [uo1] = many; extra

我想攞一杯大杯咖啡，攞糖，唔攞奶。
[ngoi1 lhieng2 huo2 yid2-boi1 ai3 boi1 ga1-fie2, huo2 hong4, m4 huo2 nai5]
I would like a large (cup of) coffee; I want sugar (but) no milk.

As you can see, the conjunction "and" is not always necessary in Chinese. When you want to connect two nouns, you can use "同 (hung4)."

同 [hung4] = and

咖啡 [ga1-fie2] + 同 [hung4] + 奶茶 [nai5-ca4] = coffee and milk tea

幾錢 [gei2-ten42] = how much money

number + 蚊 [mun2] = ... dollar(s)
3 [lham1] + 蚊 [mun2] = 3 dollars

Vocabulary C 🔊

菠蘿包 [buo1-luo4 bao1] = pineapple bun
叉燒包 [ca1-sieu1 bao1] = roast pork bun
腸仔包 [cieng4-doi2 bao1] = hot dog bun
粟米包 [lhug2-mai2 bao1] = corn bun
蛋糕 [an3-gao1] = cake
蛋撻 [an3-tad2] = egg tart

Sample Sentences C 🔊

我想攞一杯大杯咖啡同菠蘿包。
[ngoi1 lhieng2 huo2 yid2-boi1 ai3 boi1 ga1-fie2 hung4 buo1-luo4 bao1]
I would like a large (cup of) coffee and a pineapple bun.

我想攞一杯大杯奶茶同叉燒包。
[ngoi1 lhieng2 huo2 yid2-boi1 ai3 boi1 nai5-ca4 hung4 ca1-sieu1 bao1]
I would like a large (cup of) milk tea and a roast pork bun.

你攞唔攞蛋撻?
[nei1 huo2 m4 huo2 an3-tad2]
Would you like some egg tarts?

> To ask a yes/no question, you can use the "verb + 唔 (m4) + verb" structure, for example, 攞唔攞 (huo2 m4 huo2), "do you want or not want," 吃唔吃 (hieg1 m4 hieg1), "do you eat or not eat," or 鍾唔鍾意 (jung1 m4 jung1-yi1) "do you like or not like."

佢鍾意吃腸仔包嘅腸仔。
[kui1 jung1-yi1 hieg1 cieng4-doi2 bao1 ge1 cieng4-doi2]
He/she likes to eat the hot dog in the hot dog bun.

Recognizing Chinese Characters

大 [ai3] = large; big
中 [jung1] = middle; medium; center
小 [lhieu2] = small

Note that the character for "small" is "小 (lhieu2)," which is different than the "細 (lhai1)" that we learned before. Although they mean the same thing, "細 (lhai1)" is acceptable as "small" in spoken Taishanese, while "小 (lhieu2)" is acceptable as standard written Chinese, Chinese characters that you will read in newspapers, any academic or professional setting.

Sample Conversation

你好,我想攞一杯細杯咖啡同中杯珍珠奶茶。
[nei1-hao2, ngoi1 lhieng2 huo2 yid2-boi1 lhai1 boi1 ga1-fie2 hung4 jung1 boi1 jin1-ji1 nai5-ca4]
Hi, I would like a small (cup of) coffee and a medium (cup of) bubble tea.

Amy

Staff

咖啡攞唔攞糖同奶？
[ga1-fie2 huo2 m4 huo2 hong4 hung4 nai5?]
(Do you) want sugar and milk in the coffee?

我攞奶，唔攞糖。
[ngoi1 huo2 nai5, m4 huo2 hong4]
I want milk (and) no sugar.

Amy

Staff

好，唔該你等下。
[hao2, m4-goi1 nei1 ang2 ha5]
Okay, please wait a second.

幾錢啊？
[gei2-ten42 a1?]
How much is it?

Amy

Staff

6蚊。
[lug3 mun2]
Six dollars.

唔該。
[m4-goi1]
Thank you.

Amy

A beginner's guide to mastering conversational Taishanese

Cultural Insights | What do you say when you receive a compliment?

Humility is considered a virtue in many East Asian cultures, and therefore it is considered polite to downplay yourself when someone gives you a compliment. When someone gives you a compliment, you can simply say "乃啊 (nai52 a1)?" Although this literally means "Where is it?," it expresses the speaker's humility by implying, "How am I good enough?"

You may feel a little uneasy downplaying yourself after working hard to achieve something, but here are two very practical benefits of being humble:
1. To make yourself appear less threatening to others.
2. When you make a mistake, no one can blame you because you never claimed to be good at it.

See answers on page #119

Chapter 9 Exercises

1. When do you use 兩 (lieng2) for "two"?

   _____

2. When do you use 二 (ngei3) for "two"?

   _____

3. What is the word that expresses both "excuse me" (for attention) and "thank you" (for service)?

   _____

4. What is the classifier for a beverage that means "a cup of …"?

   _____

5. Translate the following sentences:

   [ngoi1 lhieng2 huo2 yid2-boi1 jin1-ji1 nai5-ca4]
   我想攞一杯珍珠奶茶。

   _____

   [ngoi1 lhieng2 huo2 lieng2-boi1 ai3 boi1 jin1-ji1 nai5-ca4]
   我想攞兩杯大杯珍珠奶茶 。

   _____

   [jin1-ji1 nai5-ca4 lhei1 mun2]
   珍珠奶茶4蚊。

   _____

6. Fill in the blanks.

   A: What would you like?

   B: [ngoi1 lhieng2 huo2 yid2-goi1 _____ _____ _____]
   我想攞一個粟米包。
   I would like a corn bun.

7. Do you know how to say the following amounts in Taishanese?

   $8 _____

   $14 _____

   $48 _____

Part III Review

- The word for medicine is 藥 (yieg5).
- The phrase for taking medicine is 吃藥 (hieg1 yieg5).
- These = 該尼 (koi5-nai2)
- Those = 嚀尼 (nen5-nai2)
- To tell someone that you need to do something, you say, "我要 (ngoi1 yieu1) ..., I have to ...."
- To tell someone where you work, you can say, "我到…返工 (ngoi1 ao1 … fan1-gung1)."
- The verb for riding public transportation is "搭 (ab1) to ride".
- Street = 街 (gai5)
- Avenue = 大道 (ai3-ao3)
- To order a beverage, you say, "一杯 (yid2-boi1) one cup of …."
- When you don't want something in your food, you can say, "唔攞 (m4 huo2) … I don't want …."
- One way to ask a yes/no question is to add 嗎 (ma1) at the end of a statement, for example, "你吃 (nei1 hieg1) you eat" + "嗎 (ma1)" becomes, "Do you (want to) eat?"
- Another way to ask a yes/no question is to use "verb + 唔 (m4) + verb" structure, for example, "你吃唔吃 (nei1 hieg1 m4 hieg1)", "Do you (want to) eat?"
- To ask how much something is, you can say, "幾錢 (gei2-ten42) how much?"
- … dollars = …蚊 (mun2)

偙媽到6大道29街返工。佢到唐人街住,要搭B車返工。唐人街嘅菠蘿包好好吃。你想吃嗎?
[ngoi5 ma2 ao1 lug3 ai3-ao3 ngei3-sib3-giu2 gai52 fan1-gung1. kui1 ao1 hong4-ngin4 gai5 ji3, yieu1 ab1 bi2 cie1 fan1-gung1. hong4-ngin4 gai5 ge1 buo1-luo4 bao1 hao2 hao2-hieg1. nei1 lhieng2 hieg1 ma1?]

English Translation:
My mom works on 6th Avenue and 29th Street. She lives in Chinatown, (and she) takes the B train to go to work. Chinatown's pineapple buns are very delicious. Do you want to eat?

Sample Exercises

Answer the following questions about yourself.

你到乃返工? [nei1 ao1 nai52 fan1-gung1?]

_____

你搭乜車返工? [nei1 ab1 mod2 cie1 fan1-gung1?]

_____

你該時想吃乜? [nei1 koi5-si52 lhieng2 hieg1 mod2?]

_____

Chapter 10

Journaling: past, present, and future
寫日記：過去、現在、將來
(lhie2 ngid3-gei12: guo1-hui1, yen3-doi3, dieng1-loi4)

As you've seen in previous chapters, watching your loved ones experience memory loss is painful. So in Chapter 10, I am writing a journal about this past summer with Popo to make sure we record these memories in words. I am writing about the past, present, and future in my journal. After reading this journal, you will be able to use different participles to indicate whether an event happened in the past, present, or future.

A beginner's guide to mastering conversational Taishanese

Simple Past

verb + 誒 [e1] = ...ed
來 [loi4] = to come
來誒 [loi4 e1] = came

Vocabulary A 🔊

Verb	English	Verb with Past Participle	English
[mai1] 買	to buy	[mai1 e1] 買誒	bought
[ngim2] 飲	to drink	[ngim2 e1] 飲誒	drank
[m4 gei1-ag1] 唔記得	to forget; to not remember	[m4 gei1-ag1 e1] 唔記得誒	forgot
[hui1] 去	to go	[hui1 e1] 去誒	went

Cultural Notes

If you simply say, "佢去誒 (kui1 hui1 e1) he/she went," in Taishanese, without specifying where "he/she" went, it can imply that this person has passed away. This is similar to the English phrase, "He/she passed." To avoid misunderstandings or accidentally crossing into Chinese taboo territory, always say where the person went if you use the verb "去 (hui1) to go" in Taishanese.

Sample Sentences A 🔊

我買誒朱古力。[ngoi1 mai1 e1 ji1-gu2-led2]
I bought chocolate.

你頭先去誒乃? [nei1 heu4-lhen12 hui1 e1 nai52?]
Where did you go before?

我今日吃誒粟米包。[ngoi1 gim1-ngid5 hieg1 e1 lhug2-mai2 bao1]
I ate (a) corn bun today.

我唔記得誒。[ngoi1 m4 gei1-ag1 e1]
I forgot.

佢去誒廁所。[kui1 hui1 e1 lhu1-suo2]
He/she went to the bathroom.

Present Progressive

Verb + 緊 [gin2] = ...ing
來緊 [loi4 gin2] = coming

Vocabulary B

Verb	English	Verb with Past Participle	English
[hieng1] 聽	to listen	[hieng1 gin2] 聽緊	listening
[du1] 做	to do	[du1 gin2] 做緊	doing
[mun3] 問	to ask	[mun3 gin2] 問緊	asking
[hog3] 學	to learn	[hog3 gin2] 學緊	learning

Sample Sentences B

我聽緊音樂。[ngoi1 hieng1 gin2 yim1-ngog3]
I am listening to music.

偘妹做緊作業。[ngoi5 moi5 du1 gin2 dog2-ngieb3]
My younger sister is doing homework.

佢問緊老師。[kui1 mun3 gin2 lao2-lhu1]
He/she is asking the teacher.

Note that 係 (hai3) is not used here before the verb.

Future

會 [voi5] + verb = will...
會來 [voi5 loi4] = will come

Vocabulary C

Verb	English	Verb with Present Participle	English
[hai2] 睇	to look; to watch; to read	[voi5 hai2] 會睇	will watch
[bong1] 幫	to help	[voi5 bong1] 會幫	will help
[nam2] 諗	to think	[voi5 nam2] 會諗	will think
[jen2] 整	to make	[voi5 jen2] 會整	will make

Sample Sentences C

我天早會睇書。[ngoi1 hen4-dao2 voi5 hai2 si1]
I will read books tomorrow.

唔使愁,我會幫你。[m4 soi2 seu4, ngoi1 voi5 bong1 nei1]
Don't worry, I will help you.

我會諗下。[ngoi1 voi5 nam2 ha5]
I will think about it a little bit.

我會整蛋糕。[ngoi1 voi5 jen2 an3-gao1]
I will make a cake.

Comparisons

Verb	...ed	...ing	will...
[du1] 做	[du1 e1] 做誒	[du1 gin2] 做緊	[voi5 du1] 會做
[hai2] 睇	[hai2 e1] 睇誒	[hai2 gin2] 睇緊	[voi5 hai2] 會睇
[hog3] 學	[hog3 e1] 學誒	[hog3 gin2] 學緊	[voi5 hog3] 會學

Recognizing Chinese Characters

日 [ngid1/ngid5] = day; sun
去 [hui1] = to go
做 [du1] = to do

Sample Diary 🔊

該個暑假好特別。[koi5-goi1 si2-ga2 hao2 ag3-bed3]
This summer vacation was very special.

我同婆婆去誒飲茶，偋吃誒好多蝦餃。
[ngoi1 hung4 puo4-puo42 hui1 e1 ngim2-ca4, ngoi5 hieg1 e1 hao2-uo1 ha5-gao2]
Popo and I went to dim sum (and) we ate many shrimp dumplings.

婆婆鍾意聽音樂，我好鍾意同佢跳舞。
[puo4-puo42 jung1-yi1 hieng1 yim1-ngog3, ngoi1 hao2 jung1-yi1 hung4 kui1 hieu1-mu2]
Popo likes to listen to music, and I really like to dance with her.

有時佢唔記得誒係禮拜幾，有時佢唔記得誒我係誰。
[yiu1-si52 kui1 m4 gei1-ag1 e1 hai3 lai5-bai1 gei2, yiu1-si52 kui1 m4 gei1-ag1 e1 ngoi1 hai3 sui52]
At times, she forgot what day of the week it was, (and) sometimes she forgot who I was.

我會話，『我係你嘅孫。』[ngoi1 voi5 va3, ngoi1 hai3 nei1 ge1 lhun1]
I would tell her, "I am your grandchild."

有一日，佢會完全唔記得我係誰。
[yiu1-yid2-ngid1, kui1 voi5 yon4-tun4 m4 gei1-ag1 ngoi1 hai3 sui52]
One day, she will completely forget who I am.

但係我會記得佢。[an3-hai3 ngoi1 voi5 gei1-ag1 kui1]
But I will remember her.

Cultural Insights | Lunar Calendar

Today, most countries in the world use the Gregorian calendar, including the U.S. and China. However, China adopted the Gregorian calendar only after Sun Yat-sen founded the Republic of China in 1912. Most Chinese traditional festivals are still based on the lunar calendar, because it has had a much longer history in China. Well-known Chinese festivals such as the Spring Festival (Chinese New Year), Mid-Autumn Festival, and Qingming Festival (Tomb-Sweeping Festival) are based on the lunar calendar. In addition, the twelve Chinese zodiac signs are also based on the lunar calendar.

十六日 = the 16th day of the month in the lunar calendar

See answers on page #118

Chapter 10 Exercises

1. Does Chinese have tenses?

   _____

2. Which participle do you add after a verb to indicate an event happened in the past?

   _____

3. Which participle do you add after a verb to indicate an event is happening now?

   _____

4. Which participle do you add before a verb to indicate an event will happen in the future?

   _____

5. Translate or transliterate the following sentences:

   I am learning Taishanese.

   _____

   I ate shrimp rice noodle rolls today.

   _____

   [ngoi1 voi5 bong1 nei1]
   我會幫你。

   _____

List of Interrogative Pronouns

誰 [sui52] = who

乜 [mod2] = what

幾時 [gei2-si52] = when

乃 [nai52] = where

幾解 [gei2-gai2] = why

哪 [nai5] = which

幾浩 [gei2-hao52] = how

Answer Key

Chapter 1

1. You are good. / You are well.
2. She is my mom.

    ngoi1 hai3 nei1 ge1 nui2

    You are not his/her/their dad.

    He is your younger brother.

Chapter 2

1. m4 goi1 (唔該)
2. m4 goi1 (唔該)
3. lhieng2 huo2
4. I would like (some) shrimp dumplings.

    You want shiu-mai (steamed pork dumpling)?
5. mod2

    ngoi1 lhieng2 huo2

Chapter 3

1. ngoi1 jung1-yi1 …. (我鍾意)
2. ma1 (嗎)
3. nei1 jung1-yi1 du1 mod2? (你鍾意做乜?)
4. ngoi1 hao2 ngan2-fun1

    I like to read (books).

    Do you like to dance?

    nei1 jung1-yi1 hieng1 mod2 yim1-ngog3

Part I Review

She is my mom.

I would like (some) shrimp rice noodle rolls.

ngoi1 hao2 gui3

Chapter 4

1. lai5-bai1 (禮拜)
2. ngoi1 lai5-bai1-mei2 jung1-yi1 …. (我禮拜尾鍾意 ….)
3. My phone number is ….
4. No
5. Today is Sunday.
   hen4-dao2 hai3 lai5-bai1 gei2
   My number is 838-274-1710.
   ngoi1 ge1 hao3-ma52 hai3 bad1-lham1-yid2, lieng4-giu2-ngei3, lug3-yid2-lham1-ngei3.
   (我嘅號碼係831-092-6132。)

Chapter 5

1. year-month-day
2. No
3. nei1 ge1 sang1-ngid3 hai3 gei2-si52? (你嘅生日係幾時?)
   ngoi1 ge1 sang1-ngid3 hai3 lug3-ngud3 sib3-lhei1 hao3. (我嘅生日係六月十四號。)
   Today is Sept. 16, 2024.
4. lhei1-sib3-ng2
   gim1-ngid5

Chapter 6

1. tieg1 (赤)
2. ngoi1 heu4 tieg1. (我頭赤。)
3. ngoi1 m4 si1-fug3. (我唔舒服。)
4.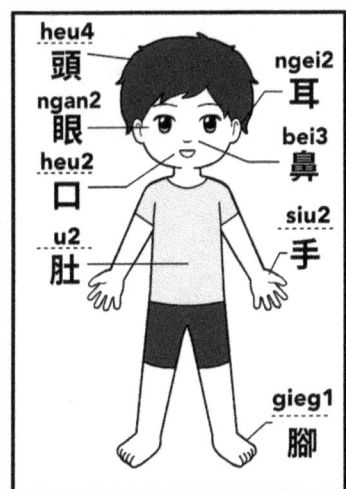

5. He/she has a fever.
   I have a vaccine shot on Thursday.
   Do you have a sore throat?

Part II Review
   tid2 ngud3 ngei3-sib3-ng2 hao3 (七月二十五號)
   kui1 dam5-man52 heu4 tieg1 (佢昨晚頭赤。)
   ngoi1 m4 ei1-tui4 nei1 sug3 mod2 (我唔a隨你屬乜。)

Chapter 7
1. hieg1 (吃)
2. ngim2 (飲)
3. lib1 (粒)
4. yid2-ngid1 … lhu1 (一日…次)
5. You take the cough medicine.
   He/she takes the medicine three times a day.
   yid2-lhu1 hieg1 lhei1-lib1 (一次吃四粒。)

6.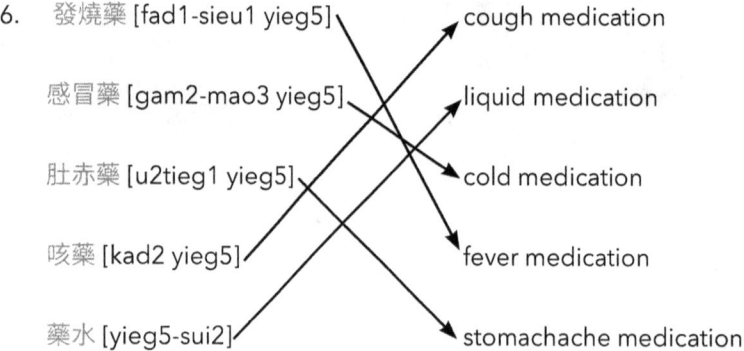

   發燒藥 [fad1-sieu1 yieg5] — cough medication
   感冒藥 [gam2-mao3 yieg5] — liquid medication
   肚赤藥 [u2tieg1 yieg5] — cold medication
   咳藥 [kad2 yieg5] — fever medication
   藥水 [yieg5-sui2] — stomachache medication

Chapter 8
1. ao1 (到)
2. nei1 ao1 nai52 ji3? (你到乃住?)
3. hong4-ngin4-gai5 (唐人街)
4. I worked./I went to work before.
   I take the B train to go to school.
   Where do you work?
5. ngoi1 ab1 kiu2 cie1 fan1-gung1

Chapter 9

1. when you quantify something
2. when you are counting
3. m4-goi1 (唔該)
4. boi1 (杯)
5. I would like a (cup of) bubble tea.
   I would like two large (cups of) bubble tea.
   The bubble tea is four dollars.
6. lhug2-mai2 bao1
7. bad1 mun2
   sib3-lhei1 mun2
   lhei1-sib3-bad1 mun2

Part III Review

Sample answer

1. ngoi1 ao1 sib3-lhei1 gai52 (14th Street) fan1-gung1.
2. ngoi1 ab1 di2 cie1 (D train) fan1-gung1.
3. ngoi1 koi5-si52 lhieng2 hieg1 lai1-men3 (ramen).

Chapter 10

1. No
2. e1 (誒)
3. gin2 (緊)
4. voi5 (會)
5. ngoi1 hog3 gin2 hoi4-san1-va32 (我學緊台山話。)
   ngoi1 gim1-ngid5 hieg1 e1 ha5-cieng42 (我今日吃誒蝦腸。)
   I will help you.

References

"China Puts a Roof on Housing Prices to Contain a Red Hot Property Market." By Stella Yifan Xie and Chong Koh Ping. The Wall Street Journal. New York, 9 June 2021.

Deng, Jun 鄧鈞. *Taishanhua Gaiyao* 台山話概要. Hunan: Hunan Electronic and Audio-visual Publishing House, 2020. Print.

Chin, Gene M. *Hoisanva English Dictionary*. Mar. 2021. Web. 10 June 2021.

Li, Stephen. *Taishanese Dictionary & Resources*. Web. 10 June 2021.

Liu, Lening 劉樂寧. "Chinese syntax and morphology." Teaching Chinese to Students of Other Languages. Beijing Language and Culture University. Jul. 2016. Lecture.

"Taishanese." Wikipedia. Wikimedia, n.d. Web. 17 June 2021.

Tang, Sze-Wing 鄧思穎. *Lecture on Cantonese Grammar*. Hong Kong: The Commercial Press, July 2015. Print.

Acknowledgements

For a book that takes years to complete, I can say without a doubt that there have been more than a handful of moments when I wanted to give up. I was very fortunate to have met many, *many* people who not only constantly encouraged me to persevere, but also provided me with valuable resources to teach Taishanese, a dialect forgotten by many but treasured by you.

To **my students in Taishanese**, you were truly the motivators for me to write and teach Taishanese. Thank you for venturing into this language desert with me so that we might one day bring streams of resources back here to benefit others.

To **Michelle Cusick**, thank you for allowing me to witness the vulnerability behind the challenges brought by language barriers and the strength of the family bonds that blossomed within these struggles. I knew I wasn't a great teacher of Taishanese at first, yet you were very patient with me and welcomed everything I had to say.

To **Edmond Xu**, for your passion and effort to preserve and advocate for Taishanese. Your generosity and humility amazes and motivates me to keep sharing the language we love with others.

To **Brittany Chan and Jared Vucina**, for not only your faithful reminders of the importance of my work, but also the valuable resources and advice you shared with me to create Taishanese video content through *Taishanese Stories with Jade*.

To **Kimberly Newell**, for always supporting the work I do and the causes I care about. Your curiosity for learning and attention to detail never cease to amaze me.

To **June Pham**, for the simple and structured layout design that makes the book fun and engaging for readers. Your never-ending encouragement and diligence motivate me to constantly grow and make progress on each book we work on together.

To **Carmen Yeung**, not only for editing this book, but also for being a great friend who always patiently listens and understands my words beyond their literal meaning.

To **Tina Gee**, for your thoughtful design and style, which shines through every beautiful illustration you did in this book. This book would not be complete without your work and spirit.

To **Poupeh Missaghi**, my first reader for this book. Your passion to learn about my language and culture means just as much to me as your edits. When I saw how your eyes sparkled while reading early drafts, I was reinvigorated to bring both fun and educational content to my readers.

To **Mike Liu**, thanks for being a great storyteller and always welcoming me to visit your lovely mom. Her story will live forever and inspire many others.

To the **Baruch Writing Center**, for the resources provided to me while editing my early drafts.

To **Hoisan Sauce**, for being such a deeply supportive group of friends on my journey to advocate for Taishanese. You are the ones that I always turn to for Taishanese learning resources.

To **Ewen Lee**, for generously offering your expertise in linguistics and Chinese.

To **Jasmine Xu**, for your weekly reminders to write and revise. You gave life to my first book with your beautiful illustrations so that I can continue writing.

To **Alison Cohen**, my lifelong teacher, friend, and inspiration, for your kindness and encouragement. Thank you for constantly reminding me of the joy I find in teaching and following my heart to continue writing.

Finally, **to my parents and grandparents**, who were my very first Taishanese teachers and still teach me something new in Taishanese each day. I feel so blessed to have families who endlessly support the pursuit of my passion and never once doubted my career path. This book belongs to you.

About the Author

Photo credit: Michelle Cusick

Jade Jia Ying Wu completed her Teaching Certificate Program in TESOL (Teaching English to Speakers of Other Languages) and TCSOL (Teaching Chinese to Speakers of Other Languages) from Teachers College, Columbia University and Beijing Language and Culture University in 2016. She has taught Chinese in classrooms of various sizes and to students of all ages, in both the U.S. and China. She holds a bachelor's degree in statistics and quantitative modeling from Baruch College, City University of New York.

Jade was born and raised in Taishan, Guangdong, China, where Taishanese is the mainstream dialect. She moved to Swartz Creek, Michigan at the age of thirteen and spent most of her young adulthood living in New York City. Experiencing both Chinese and American cultures, she was often confused yet fascinated by the differences between them. In 2014, she created her website Inspirlang to teach Cantonese, Mandarin, and Taishanese to non-native and heritage speakers, and developed her own romanized system for Taishanese. She currently hosts language podcasts such as *Learn Taishanese Daily*, *Learn Cantonese Daily*, and *Cantonese Diaspora*. A former instructor at CUNY, she is also the author of both the *Learn to Speak Cantonese* and *Learn to Speak Mandarin* book series.

In her free time, Jade also enjoys hiking, jogging, and learning other languages. She lives in Brooklyn, New York.

www.inspirlang.com
www.inspirlang.com/rssfeed

@InspirLang

More from Jade

Learn to Speak Cantonese 1
Paperback and ebook available

Imagine falling in love with someone, but not speaking the same language as their extended family. This is the case for Gabriel, the narrator of this textbook, who is an American boy learning Cantonese to impress his girlfriend's mom. In this Cantonese learning book, you will join Gabriel in his first meeting with Jenny's mother, who is from Hong Kong and can only speak Cantonese. From having dim sum to describing his favorite pastimes, Gabriel will teach you everything you need to know to master basic conversational Cantonese.

Learn to Speak Cantonese 2
Paperback and ebook available

It is not easy to leave one's comfort zone to learn a new language and adapt to a new culture, as you might have learned from Gabriel in Book 1. In Book 2 of the *Learn to Speak Cantonese* series, meet Ben, a polar bear, who's starting an adventure with his best friend, Stormy, a Pomeranian dog. Together, the two are traveling to Hong Kong to advocate for green living! In this book, you will join Ben and Stormy as they spend twelve months living in Hong Kong and learning how to use Cantonese in everyday life.

Learn to Speak Mandarin 1
Paperback and ebook available

Imagine you have found your dream job at a company that is located in a different country, but you don't speak the language of that country. This is the case for An An, the narrator of this textbook. An An is a brave panda from Washington, D.C. who learned Mandarin and traveled across the world to Beijing for his dream job interview. In this book, you will join An An for 10 hours (chapters) for his first day in Beijing going to his job interview and learning to speak Chinese in a variety of settings.

www.ingramcontent.com/pod-product-compliance
Lightning Source LLC
Chambersburg PA
CBHW080415170426
43194CB00015B/2813